WHO NEEDS CANTONA WHEN WE'VE GOT...

DEDICATIONS

I dedicate this book to all those wonderful Sunderland fans out there, my Mam and Dad who have stood by me whatever, my three wonderful kids who I am so proud of; Liam, Jessica and Charlie, the rest of my family, but most of all my Gran; I think of you every day.

ACKNOWLEDGEMENTS

Pratty and Owersy, thanks for being like brothers to me. Andrew, thanks for putting up with my stuttering dribble! Sincere thanks also to the following; Aidy, Quinny, Rob Mason, Paul Briggs at twocan, Rob Metcalfe, Austin Carney and everybody else at Durham City AFC and Soccarena and lastly, Sunderland AFC; for letting me be on your books for 14 years.

Richard Ord

Sincere thanks to my family and friends, and my wife Miranda in particular, for all your support, and to Andrew Bousfield, Paul Briggs, Michael Cassley and Rob Mason, for your welcome guidance.

Andrew Smithson

a twocan publication

© Richard Ord 2012.
Published by twocan.

ISBN 978-0-9573473-2-8

I remember discussing the idea with my wife when I was first approached to help Dickie Ord write this book, when she asked the question of whether I personally would want to even read such a title. The answer was, of course, a resounding yes.

Dickie grew up supporting Sunderland. Twenty years or so later, when he was fulfilling his childhood dreams and playing for the club he loved, I was busy falling in love with it too, and some of the games and memories in these pages formed not only his career but my childhood too.

Had I not received the call Dickie was always guaranteed at least one sale therefore, but I have been privileged enough however to be more than a reader and working with Dickie and talking at length, not only about that time at Sunderland but also his fascinating experiences on the wrong end of footballing fate in the capital and the harsh realities of the game at grass roots level in his native County Durham, has been an absolute joy.

When Dickie made his debut on 3rd November 1987 Sunderland were starting on the long road to recovery after reaching their lowest ebb. Roker Park, much loved but showing sings of its age, was playing host to third tier football for the first time in its history and a once proud club was coming to terms with its fall from grace.

Manager Denis Smith was making inroads however and the 7-0 thrashing handed out to Southend United was even more remarkable given the fact that at the heart of defence was a raw 17 year old, one of a clutch of local players that in the following decade tried to help the club keep pace within the world of football.

By the time he made his final appearance eleven years later Dickie had witnessed seismic shifts both at his own club and within the game as a whole. I hope this book finds itself onto the shelves of many a fellow fan, and that in reading it you enjoy reliving a period of great change at Sunderland and learn more about one of their most committed players ever.

Andrew Smithson

Richard 'Dickie" Ord is the quintessential 'Mackem'. His journey from passionately supporting his team from the terraces of Roker Park to becoming idolised himself by the same Sunderland faithful is a welcome reminder that Premiership football isn't exclusively tailored to over paid, undedicated players short on loyalty.

Dickie's ability as a polished ball playing defender was sublime. For that he is rightly respected throughout the game but in attempting to describe his finest quality, namely his incredible passion for Sunderland Association Football Club, I have to do it via another North East sporting giant; Durham County Cricket Club.

My first trip as a Sunderland player in August 1996 took me for a midweek fixture away to Nottingham Forest.

It's just after lunch in a twin bed hotel room, scene of the customary afternoon nap ahead of the evening game. I pull the curtains to block out daylight and ask my new room partner would he like to watch TV for a while. I kindly hand him the remote;

"I'll put the cricket on" states Dickie.

"I didn't know there was any on today?" I reply.

"Teletext son, you can't beat watching a good days cricket on the Teletext, especially when the Durham lads are oot."

I smiled, shook my head, and then got into my single bed - closing my eyes and thinking of nothing more but supplementing my ego with a goal or two that evening. With no sound, no lights and only a silent Teletext page capturing the attention of my partner it should have been a blissful sleep.

It was anything but. The constant applause each time a page rolled stating a single run had occurred and his hollering "gan on me son" as silent news of a silent boundary took place eventually led to confrontation;

"Any chance Richard, we've a big game tonight?"

"Me names Dickie and are yee questioning me preparation bonny lad?"

"No, just mine actually."

"Are yee saying I'm not dedicated like Mr Billy Big Time?"

"If it's half as good as your dedication to invisible cricket then I'm sure you'll be fine."

"Listen, when yee have earned the right to tell a Mackem to switch the telly off I'll gladly do it, but for now yee are just another one of those journey men who come to my club, go through the motions, take the money and run."

I was taken aback but straight away I knew he had challenged me professionally. It was my first lesson in North East football passion and I quickly took it on board. I backed off, nodded respectfully and thought to myself, 'Well bonny lad, if it's passion you want you've come to the right man.'

That very afternoon my love affair with Sunderland kicked off. That was the day I 'got' the Mackem way, the day I knew Sunderland was a special club and the right place for me. Thanks Ordy.

You know, I have to thank him for a lot more than just giving me the Mackem bug though. Over time I came to befriend his closest pals from Murton and Seaham, two areas renowned for their wacky characters (Dickie's pals bring clear validity to that statement). Too many late nights in Big Aidy's pub didn't help either of our marriages but the memories are priceless. I shall leave it to him to tell the tales!

Having played, coached, managed and steered Sunderland from the board room I've never been certain that Dickie has fully accepted my Sunderland credentials. I guess asking me to pen this foreword should finally put me at ease but you never know with Ordy. Lavishing praise was always a rare commodity in his makeup, although I am confident enough to let every true Sunderland fan know that I believe no living soul will ever show better passion for 'our' great club than Murton's Richard Ord. Enjoy the read.

Niall Quinn

The day the revival started...

CHAPTER ONE

Oo ar, were gannin up ya knar

When Peter Reid came in to take over as manager of Sunderland it was out of the blue really; there were seven games to save us from relegation otherwise I don't think the club would have ever come back from it. The mood around the club seemed horrendous under Mick Buxton, I can remember when we did go down to the old third division, but the place seemed even lower than back then; Mick Buxton was a lovely lad, proper old school, but after starting well I felt he had ran out of steam and that we needed a boost.

Reidy's arrival was big news, he was a well known name and I remember when he first came into the changing room everybody was a bit in awe of him. He just made sure everybody was relaxed though, and after training he got us all in and said "right, I'm taking you all out tomorrow".

This was on the Tuesday and on the Wednesday we all went down to The Cantonese Palace in Seaburn, which for a manager to arrange was new to all of us. He ordered a load of food, a load of drink, and we had a great afternoon; it put everybody at ease. He rang me the day after that meal and because of my strong accent was taking the water and said "I thought you were French", but he put his arm around me and that was it for us two. He did that with a lot of players, it's man management.

Mick would always try and have meetings before games, especially when we were away from home, and he would sit us down for an hour and a half in the hotel and tell us about how this bloke walked, what he was good at, what he wasn't good at, rather than concentrating on ourselves, and we felt like he was putting us down. Reidy was all about what we were going to do and said 'go and express yourselves'. It was a complete change, a relief really.

We were playing Sheffield United in Reidy's first game and it was very tense. Because I had done well in training Reidy had rang my old coach Viv Busby to talk about me and Viv had told him to stick me in the team, and everything kicked on from there. We won the game 1-0 after Craig Russell scored, the keeper had got a hand on the shot but Russ had stuck it powerfully so it still crossed the line in front of the Fulwell End.

We followed that with a win at Derby County but those seven games were all very close and it was only after we drew at Burnley in our penultimate game that we were mathematically safe. Turf Moor is a lovely old fashioned ground and I remember they had to put the kick off back because all of the Sunderland fans trying to get in. The delay meant we were all very edgy, but Reidy came into the dressing room and told us couple of jokes that had us all on the floor laughing and it took the tension away in an instant; he had provided the lift everybody at the club needed and we started playing with a bit of confidence.

After going so close to relegation though Reidy knew there was more to do, so the following pre season was spent in Ireland and it was as much about team spirit as it was getting fit. After playing Shamrock Rovers Reidy said that we could go out, with a curfew of two o'clock, so we were all like 'wow, a two o'clock curfew in pre season!' We all got showered and changed and there was a big bus waiting outside for us because we were going out a few miles down the road. Reidy came out and there was this big limo right next to the bus waiting for him and as he was getting in he called "see you lads, Sacko; you're in charge!"

Reidy had brought Bobby Saxton in and I loved Sacko, I still do, and he was one of the reasons why I did so well that following season. He is great craic and we ended up having a brilliant night; a two o'clock curfew during pre season was also unheard of, so by about one o'clock a few had already gone back to the hotel. With me being conscientious and trying to stay on with the new manager, come the end of the night I said to the last few "ha'way lads, we're going to have be going" and they were like 'nah nah, leave it out Dickie' so after trying to persuade them for a while I ended up having to run back and got in to the hotel at one minute past two, and there's Sacko waiting for me at reception; he never said anything though and just started laughing.

The other lads were still out and they came back at five o' clock in the morning, but Sacko had gone to bed by then. When I got up in the morning Kevin Ball told me the gaffer wanted to see me, so he came with me and Reidy was just sat there drinking a cup of tea. I start saying "look gaffer, I'm sorry" and he just started laughing too. I thought I was going to get fined or sacked or something, but he just said "Dickie, don't worry; just buy all the lads a bottle of wine or something" and that was it. Reidy was one of them; if you worked hard for him in training and in games you bought yourself a bit of freedom, even though the lads that stayed out never got found out!

That pre season we played a few games, and because all of Reidy's family are over there we were going to local boozers all the time and honestly, after every match it was 'get yourselves out lads' and when people talk about the team spirit we had then it all came about from that, and Reidy made it to be honest.

We never did a single run whilst we were over there - I remember one pre season Mick had us running up Silksworth Ski Slope when Terry Butcher was manager and he was saying "this will do you good in November lads, this will get you through it" and its probably one of the reasons why I've now got a bad back! Under Reid everything was all high intensity with the ball and Sacko would do a lot of it; the training, the team talks. They were very straight forward and both used to say, 'football is a simple game, all it is about is what happens when we've got the ball, and when they've got the ball'.

Sacko's first ever coaching session was warming up with the ball, which was a new idea then, and we played 15 a side on a big pitch so it was tight, two touch, and we then played three team possession. It was brilliant, we all had a laugh and that's what you want as footballers, trying to have a bit of fun and not letting it drag on as I felt it could with Mick. He would bring us back in for afternoons and I even remember him trying to coach Martin Smith of all people one time how to take in swinging corners for about an hour and a half when it as chucking down and the rest of us were all lying down on the ground freezing to death. Things like that used to just make you think 'what's he talking about'. Then it went from one extreme to the other with Sacko and Reidy; short and sharp.

Things like that make a difference, that pre season summed it up and we carried the mood on into the season, although I don't think we started all that well to be honest, so had to have that spirit to get through it. When we were losing 2-0 at home to Preston North End in the League Cup Reidy absolutely laid into us at half time, I don't think we were not trying for him but it just wasn't clicking and Lee Howey's goals in the second half were pivotal. We won the game 3-2 but if Lee hadn't have gone and done that Reidy had spoken about making wholesale changes, so it kept us together and obviously we kicked on from there.

It's rare now that somebody can drift out of the professional game and come back in but Lee was like Ian Sampson, 'Sammo' signed from Goole Town and we played a lot together for the reserves. Lee was playing semi professionally for Seaham Red Star then went abroad and Terry Butcher brought him back. Lee was at Ipswich Town with him at one time but he was great to have in the squad, and he did get the odd vital goal as well. He is a lovely lad and I used to room with him a lot.

Towards the end of the year we were becoming very hard to beat and of course a lot of people remember the game against Millwall in early December. They were top of the table yet we beat them 6-0; Russ scored four but I played well too. I was captain for that match so it gave me great satisfaction; my son Liam was born in the March the previous year and Kevin Ball was over the moon at the time because he said it would be the making of me. Bally was right because Liam was starting to grow and you settle down, or you try to anyway, and I had just captained Sunderland as they hit top spot in Division One.

We were struggling a bit through Christmas however and it was a bad winter so we had lots of postponements. It meant we had plenty of games in hand over the other clubs at the top, one of which was Grimsby Town at home. Shay Given had just come into the side and he made a great one on one save in the first half that kept the scores level, but it was a dour game really; they only had that one chance and we only had one chance, which I was able to score with. Martin Scott had a free kick on the left and I think they tried to play offside so I was on my own at the back post and was able to take the ball down with my right and slot it past the keeper from a bit of an angle; it was a freezing cold night and I just went berserk! I tore off down past the Clock Stand and I couldn't run for another 20 minutes until I got my breath back, but I suppose the celebration made everybody laugh.

I didn't score many but when I did I would go off it a bit. It's everybody's dream though isn't it, particularly as I'd supported the club all of my life. You see people now who just stand there when they score, but fans have got to be able to relate to the players and football is awful at the moment because there is none of that. I think this was the last period where teams had loads of local lads in their squads and everybody knew each other. It was an important goal though because we hadn't won for six games and it was one of those where if we hadn't have won things could have started going sour.

At least we could say that two of those games had been against Manchester United in the FA Cup; both of those matches stand out obviously. They are my second team actually and I love watching them; they always have two wingers and score so many late goals. At that point Old Trafford was the only ground where you go in on the coach underneath the stadium and even doing that just gives you goose bumps. You walk out and the stands go on forever and at that time it was all about Eric

Cantona and Ryan Giggs. Giggsy was just unbelievable then and was a bit of a hero of mine.

They scored early and we thought 'here we go' but in the second half we went 2-1 up; Steve Agnew scored a good goal and then Russ put us ahead. Peter Schemeichel wasn't playing and I think he would have gobbled those efforts up really but we were quite comfortable until Lee Sharpe put a ball into the box at the far post late on. Darius Kubicki was marking Cantona and he could have easily put him off or headed it himself but he couldn't make it and the game ended 2-2. You think you'd be happy with a draw at Old Trafford but we were all distraught and I went into the changing room and I had a proper go at Darius, I had to be dragged off him. I was calling him all sorts of names because I knew he could have done better - and he knew it himself because he didn't have a go back.

The team bus was like a nightclub sometimes coming back from games and obviously the drinks were flowing after that performance. One of the directors was on with us though and had a little dig, calling us worse than useless as we were getting off, so I had to be dragged off him as well! Having a club official calling us that after we'd just drawn 2-2 at Manchester Untied was so bizarre I thought, it was unwarranted and something somebody in that position didn't need to say.

The replay was on a Tuesday night, live on Sky. The game before that was at home to Norwich City on the Sunday and that was live too on ITV. You can't turn down that sort of TV money but it did mean we had two games in three days so Reidy thought he'd keep us all together and we stayed in the Seaburn Hotel. We were thinking we'd all have to be early to bed but David Kelly got his card school going and we ended up drinking and playing cards all night. Me and Andy Melville didn't even make it to bed I don't think and come the Monday Reidy and Sacko were looking at us and just shaking their heads so decided we should just have a spa day instead of training.

It might not sound like the best preparation but sometimes it can be a benefit to switch off, and come the game Alex Ferguson changed his team because Russ and Phil 'Tippy' Gray's pace had given them a tough time at Old Trafford. He played Paul Parker at centre half but we butchered them in the first half because Reidy loved the high intensity, in your face type of performance and Tippy scored a good goal under Schemeichel. We could have even gone 2-0 ahead because Tippy hit the bar as well so we all came in at half time buzzing, but Ferguson changed it again and pushed people up front so we were hanging on in after that to be honest.

Paul Scholes scored with about 20 minutes to go - he was only young at the time and that was one of his first goals, and then Andy Cole won it in the last seconds of the game with a header across Alec Chamberlain. Cantona seemed to hate Cole, he was just hoying French expletives at him all game and Cole was giving plenty of it back to him too. People often thought that Cole had a problem with Teddy Sheringham too; but when I played against those they weren't having a go at each other, they just didn't speak at all!

I was gutted that we'd been beaten because we had performed well, but in the end they were too strong. That was the night when I done Cantona; I was having a good game and I got the ball and just went to shimmy one way then went past him and the whole stadium just started singing 'Who needs Cantona when we've got Dickie Ord'. That was the thing that stands out, because I was so proud. After the game there was always a sponsors man of the match award handed out and my favourite ever football memento, even more so than my England caps, was the magnum of champagne I was given afterwards with 'Man of the Match, Sunderland versus Manchester United' on it.

We were all in the players' lounge after the game and my best mate, Michael Pratt, was in there with me. Giggsy came into the bar and a couple of young lasses, aged about seven or eight, said "Mr Giggs, can we have your autograph" and he just said "no" and walked off. Pratty was stood at the bar and Giggsy came over to try and get served, so Pratty just burped straight in his face and said "sign that ya tosser". I didn't think Giggsy would have been like that, after all there were only a couple of them but even so, if there had been 30 or 40 you should still sign autographs if you can I think.

We were all in the lounge for a couple of hours after that; there was my Mam and Dad, all my mates, and my wife. Pratty went outside and when he came back in he said there was a "reporter from the Manchester Evening News asking if you want to speak to him" and I said "well no, not really, go and see what he wants". Pratty came back and said that the reporter was claiming Alex Ferguson was in the office with Reidy and was trying to buy me so wanted to know what I thought about it, but I replied "tell him to clear off, he's talking a load of crap".

It must have been at about 12 o'clock when we came out and this bloke was still there with Fergie's driver. He was stood at the top of the stairs and said Fergie was still in the office, and years later I found out that he did try to buy me that night and had offered Cole or Scholes plus money for me. Blackburn Rovers were after me as well but it was not the same as having Fergie interested, apparently they had been watching me all season. It's all about ifs and buts though, and I sometimes think would I have gone? Probably; anywhere else and I would have said no but you can't knock Manchester United back!

Back in the league and shortly after the Grimsby game we got battered at Wolverhampton Wanderers, but then things started going well and we started breaking a few clubs records. The Ipswich Town match stands out because they were all over us but we again showed the team spirit that was so important and still won 1-0. That game was the best Shay Given had; he saved about five one on ones because whilst he wasn't the biggest, he was able to make himself look it. George Burley, who I had played with earlier in my career, was the Ipswich manager at the time and he said afterwards that he had never seen a keeper like it. There was even one game where somebody rounded with the ball in front of the Fulwell End and he still got back up and saved it.

The Derby County game, when we beat them at Roker Park, was probably the best game I ever had for Sunderland; my old team mate Marco Gabbiadini was playing for them and I had him in my pocket. At the time we weren't scoring a lot of goals but we won 3-0 and could have scored ten. We'd been chasing them at the top of the table for a while and that made us believe in ourselves because we knew we were better than them.

I remember in that game winning a couple of tackles and I put my head up and played Paul Stewart in, he hadn't scored for us and he missed - he was devastated! He was a good lad, Stewy; very funny. He was the only one that ever took the water out of Bally, who for once didn't have an answer back! Bally's a good guy too, he's spot on, but honestly, Stewy had him in the palm of his hand. Bally was really intense about everything and took the captaincy seriously, he was proud of it. If you had a problem with anything, football, family life, he would always say 'come to me' and he was a brilliant captain on the pitch too but Stewy used to wind him up and all the lads would be in on it.

One of the lads that seemed to always be in and out of the team then was Martin Smith. It was due to injuries more than anything but I don't know if there was a problem with Reidy, who was always one of them where if he liked you he liked you and if he didn't he didn't, there was no in between. For some reason with Smithy he would be unbelievable in training but he didn't really kick on at Sunderland and maybe Reidy should have put an arm round him like he did with some of the others because Martin was one of them kids, an unbelievable talent but a real confidence player.

Martin was still playing at Sunderland RCA in the Northern League as recently as 2011 but he should have kicked on, whether it was the injuries I don't know but there is luck involved too; football can be about being at the right place at the right time. You look at Mickey Gray, Mickey probably didn't have the talent Smithy did but he had effort and work rate, loved training and rarely got injured. He's done well to have never had any major injuries and had a great career on the back of it.

When we got promoted there was Mickey, myself and Craig Russ in the studios at Tyne Tees Television; I remember stuttering on camera loads! We'd beaten Birmingham City earlier in the week and Mickey had scored a cracker that night. Barry Fry was the manager and they had a half decent side at the time but we'd been too good for them. That was one of those Roker Park nights where the atmosphere was absolutely brilliant, the lights were on, and it was a lovely night. Mickey's goal was a waxer and they just couldn't get near us. It set it up so that even though we weren't playing on the Saturday we could get promoted, so we went into the studio to watch the Crystal Palace game via a beam back and when it was confirmed that we had gone up we cheered and laughed, but I think we were a bit conscious that there were cameras on us.

The promotion party kicked off when we played the following day against Stoke City but it was another dour game, it finished 0-0 and I think I had the best chance actually; it was a volley but I stuck it into the Fulwell End. It was on ITV; but we hardly ever did well on the TV! The only game that was shown where we actually played really well was when we went to Grimsby and won 4-0. Phil Gray scored a beauty from just inside their half, and that was the game where fans started singing the 'Cheer Up Peter Reid' song and we began getting a bit of recognition.

We went away for a couple of days after that to Mottram Hall. It's quite an affluent place where lots of footballers live and Reidy used to love it; he took us there a few times. We'd just been down to Southend United too and played in thick fog where Mickey Bridges scored his first goal. I'm sure we flew there because there was a debate over whether we would come back in that weather; I couldn't even see our goals because they were at the other end of the pitch - you just heard the noise of the crowd. It wasn't too much of a problem though, me and Andy Melville never spoke to each other during the games anyway! I think we only ever had a go at each other on the pitch once, and then we started laughing afterwards anyway.

He was a one off, Mel; he knew what I was doing and I knew he what he was doing, he was such a good player and he read the game brilliantly. We played most of the games together and the back four was quite settled, and that was another factor in us getting promotion. Martin Scott was at left back and I think Scotty should have played for England; he was tremendous that year. He was a great penalty taker, had a good left foot, was quick and could read a game; what more do you want? Darius would always play on the right, I thought he was a strange bloke and he seemed to just keep himself to himself, but he still did a job for us on the pitch too.

I know it seems like there were a lot of tight, dull games that season, but we did well because we barely conceded. We had that solid back four, and two good goalkeepers, because as well as Shay you have to give Alec a mention. He was a bit unlucky to lose his place to Shay to be honest because he was a lovely bloke and we weren't conceding many at that point; but then again you can't fault Reidy for bringing Shay in either because it gave everybody a lift. When Shay left Alec stepped in again and he was brilliant, and in his first game back at Bramall Lane he pulled off a blinding save against Sheffield United.

Towards the end of the season Reidy was letting us out all of the time. The hard work had been done in training and we knew we were up. The last game of the season was against West Bromwich Albion, it was another 0-0 and I remember I had the best chance again; it was a header at the Roker End that went tamely into the keepers hands. I was captain because Bally was injured, so we came out afterwards and lifted the Division One trophy together. When I was going around the pitch with it Duncan Wood interviewed me for Tyne Tees and I pointed towards the Roker End and said "if I wasn't down here I'd be up there with my mates". There was about thirty of them in there and you couldn't get in the players lounge afterwards because it was full of all of my pals!

As well as my winner's medal I was lucky enough to be voted Player of the Season that year. I got all of them, the supporter's association one, the 'A Love Supreme' one, and they were all presented at that West Brom game. I went around all of the different suites in the Main Stand to collect these trophies and when I eventually walked into the players' lounge to meet my mates and my parents, my Dad, a man of few words, looked up and said "aye, you've had a canny season son" and that was it. Mam joked I would never get any praise from him, but to be honest I don't think I could have put it better myself. We were on our way to the Premiership barely a year after looking like going into Division Two and Reidy had made sure we did it as a team.

Roker welcomes Romania; Steaua Bucharest come to town

CHAPTER TWO

Stella Bucharest

A lot of people like to remember that 1995-96 season for a couple of reasons. We won promotion obviously, and it was one of the last periods where the fans could connect with the players; we all jumped into taxis the evening of the West Bromwich Albion game for example and went into town - everywhere was packed out with Sunderland fans, which is what it is all about. For me personally it was a memorable time too because the club had awarded me a testimonial season, although I didn't want to do it at first to be honest because I'm not that way inclined.

I don't always like to be in the limelight or to be getting lots of attention, but there was a lot of pressure put on me by different people to go ahead with it. I think my agent at the time Ian Elliott, or the Moose as we called him, reckoned it would be a money spinner but in the end I suppose it couldn't have worked out better when you consider the season we had, and it made things even more special. I hadn't always been a regular at Sunderland but that was another good thing about Reidy, he just said "you've been here all these years so you can have one, it's not a problem". Reidy was great about it all, Sacko and he helped out with it.

As a man you couldn't beat Sacko, he is one of the nicest people you will ever meet, funny as well. When you first meet him he comes over as being quite hard and cold, but he's not. He's like Reidy in one respect though; if he doesnt like you, he really doesn't like you but whenever you'd speak to the majority of the lads they all had a lot of good to say about the pair of them. Of course, with any footballer there might be the odd bad word when a decision was made that they didn't like but overall the pair gained respect and fostered the all important team spirit I have referred to by doing things such as helping out with my testimonial, even though they wouldn't have been expected too.

I approached a few of my mates to be on the committee too like Pratty, and Adrian Marshall, who joined later on. I'd first met Aidy one afternoon when he ran The Phoenix in Seaham; me, Gary Owers, Micky Harford and his brother in law Davey Hall went in and got absolutely slaughtered. Aidy gave me a lift home and me and Owers were sat in the back of his car giggling away like two school children because we were pulling the tape out of his Simply Red cassette, although he now claims it was his wife's!

When Aidy was starting to get involved it was a bit further down the line and some things had already been taken care of with regards the testimonial game, but he knew how we could do other things, like arranging non football events. We weren't doing any of it for the money though; the year was about the fans and we had some good nights, put it that way.

We didn't have things on every night, but it just seemed like every time you got over it there would be something else. Pratty lost two girlfriends during it all because it was so intense and everybody was just going mental at these nights. We set one night up in the Mill View Social Club I remember and one at Red House, and that one was absolutely choc a block. It was a crazy do; people were just diving on top of me and approaching me with their partners offering me all sorts.

We had some Sportsman's Dinners too and we'd get Bobby Knoxall on to provide entertainment so we ended up becoming really good friends. Bobby knew my

Granddad Dodi through the club land circuit, my Granddad was a singer and would get up on stage, and when I met Bobby it all came back to him. Anybody that saw Bobby perform knows that he could be a bit near the knuckle, but he would always tell some great stories.

We had a night on at Shotton Hall, and as well as Bobby we had Charlie Hurley on, but he was dying on stage. He was really struggling for some reason because normally people lap up everything he has to say, and in the end Bobby had to get up and save him. "Charlie" he said, "that goal you scored when you came up and got your head on a free kick, that's the first time I've even seen a centre half do that, do you remember that?", Charlie said "yes" so then Bobby went "and do you remember the blonde we met later that night, did you pull her?" and quick as a flash Charlie replied "no, I married her" and that completely broke the tension.

There were a lot of people there for that one and the food was good, despite the fact it was by Pat Bland Caterers. Can you believe that, Bland Caterers, what a name! All we'd made though was enough to buy a crate of champagne so we sat there drinking till six o'clock in the morning, all of my mates. There were golf days too, and a casino night down at The Ropery on the riverside, which was another waste of money. It was set up by Daryl Franklin, who ran the pub at the time and it made a bit of cash but again we drank it away that same night.

At the end of the day though whenever there was a do it was well attended and people were always making the effort to approach me, saying 'Dickie well done', shaking my hand and the rest of it, which always felt nice because it meant there was a link between us and the fans. Without them and my mates turning up for the different things they would have been a complete waste of time, but often the atmosphere ended up like being in a crowd on a match day with everybody singing and enjoying themselves.

I say mates mind, but they didn't have any problems with showing me up when they got the chance. As well as all of the nights out we had for my testimonial all the lads would still be coming to as many games as they could, but when we went to Oldham Athletic they didn't have enough tickets between them so somebody suggested that one of them tried their luck and see if they could get in by pretending to be a player. Pratty probably looked in the best shape at the time and was turned out quite well but there was another lad there, Gary Armstrong, with glasses on, wearing a long fleabag trench coat and with holes in his jeans and he pipes up saying "no, I want to go in as a player" so as the squad are going into Boundary

Park dressed in club tracksuits he follows us in and then sneaks off into the hospitality areas with the rest of the group. Then, when we are out on the pitch warming up all you can hear is him stood up in the posh seats shouting abuse at me.

The lads were trying to get him to sit down and shut up but the stewards had worked him out and decided that instead of chucking him out they would move them all into the away end and marched them along the cinder track. To get my own back I went to kick a ball at him yet he took it down brilliantly and pinged it right back to me, so to be fair to him he might have got away with pretending to be a player after all.

One of the final events we held was a night at the Rainton Meadows Arena. We had gone up by then and been handed the Division One trophy so obviously the whole place was buzzing. We were upstairs in the bar when Reidy said to me "where's the trophy Dickie? You should have it here with all the fans" and I replied "I didn't think we'd be allowed it gaffer due to the insurance and all of that", so he rang the secretary to check. Roker Park was locked but he got them to open it up, get it out from the safe and bring it across, and we stuck it on the top table so everybody could come and get photos with it. People kept breaking into choruses of 'Cheer Up Peter Reid', and then at the end of the evening Mickey Gray got up and sang the Oasis song Wonderwall and everybody was on the tables dancing; what a night it was.

Reidy didn't have to go and do that, but having the Division One trophy there made it extra special for both me and for the fans. As I said I'm not somebody that likes being in the limelight though so I felt a bit awkward at time, and obviously that night I had to stand up and thank everybody. I'm one of those that hates public speaking however so started sweating a bit and had to get through it as quickly as possible. Reidy stood up as well though and he is a brilliant speaker, so it took a bit of the attention off me.

I'm a big cricket fan and used to play with Andrew Roseberry, and his Dad would often take us both to games so Matty Roseberry and Mike Roseberry were both there on the top table as well. They run the Rainton Meadows Arena now and were good friends with John Emburey, who used to play for England, so he came along too.

At the time it was the biggest sporting dinner ever held in the north east; there was over a thousand people there. Pratty was there carrying out some committee duties and he came up to me in a panic and said "Dickie, what am I ganna dee?" so I said

19

"what's the matter son?" and he replied "come upstairs". I was at the top table so didn't think I should leave but he kept insisting, so I went up to the offices where we'd had loads of girls helping us out. They had counted out all the money and put it these plastic bags that covered the desk; I've never been a money person or had loads of cash on me, and there so much there we didn't know where to put it!

I was married at the time and I didn't get in until at about five or six in the morning. I didn't want my wife to go so I'd said there was no women allowed at this do, but obviously phone calls had been made telling her that women were there after all so when I eventually came in she was obviously annoyed, and was asking "where have you been" and all of that. I was wearing a big jacket which had all of the money inside so I opened it up and replied "that's where I've been" and dumped all of the cash on the floor. I took it down to the bank as soon as it opened but all that cash, it was just ridiculous, and yet I was still in the dog house after that!

It wasn't long after we'd had another falling out so it wasn't that much of a surprise that I was in trouble. I was third in the North East Player of the Year the season we went up and there was another do at one of the big hotels in Newcastle. It was a dickie bow tie job in the week leading up to the West Brom game and obviously lots of the Sunderland players and coaching staff went along. Everybody was telling me that I'd won the overall award, but even though I don't tend to pay much attention to things like that I was still worried that I might have to get up and give a speech.

Roger Tames was presenting the evening and Bryan Robson was handing the different trophies out and as the presentations went on I was asking myself 'what am I going to say' over and over again and getting really worked up. Of course, after all of that I didn't win it, and in a way coming third was a bit of a relief; and I still got a plaque and a big bottle of brandy awarded to me so I was over the moon. Les Ferdinand won it and Paul Bracewell got second in the end and we all stayed in the hotel till the early hours of the next day.

People started drifting off home but there was still a good few of us left; I think there was me, Reidy, Sacko, Bryan Robson, Viv Anderson, who was Robson's assistant at Middlesbrough at the time, Roger and his missus, Mel, Bally, Scotty and a couple of the other usual suspects and it was great craic.

Again, I didn't get back into the house until about six o' clock in the morning but I hadn't let go of the plaque once since I had been presented with it. We'd bought our first house together in East Rainton and Liam was still only a little bairn at the time so I remember that because it was light outside and the birds were singing I'd thought I should creep in and try not to wake anybody. I was thinking to myself 'I'm in big trouble here' so I went onto the sofa and pretended to have fallen asleep, but Sonia heard me moving around so she came down and in all the carry on the plaque got dropped and damaged. I was distraught at the time but I've still got it now.

As for the testimonial game itself we'd had Middlesbrough all sorted but the police contacted us a few weeks before it was supposed to be played to say that they were no longer willing to give it the go ahead. It would have been a sell out, but they'd changed their minds and explained they were worried about the possibility of crowd bother. Three years before that when Glasgow Rangers came down for Gary Bennett's testimonial there was absolute hell on in the town with all the Scots, so at the last minute we ended up with Steaua Bucharest instead, who had been in the Champions League the previous season. My agent thought they would be attractive opposition but it never took off and in the end I made more the night we had a do at the Rainton Meadows.

With it being so short notice Steaua were badly organised and the whole thing was a mess really. When they got here they'd found out that there was no training pitch available so we tried everybody; we rang the council, we rang Newcastle United, and not even Sunderland would give them anywhere to work out at. None of the local non league football clubs that we tried would help and we even rang a couple of schools, but because this was all happening on a Friday night they had nobody available even when we offered to pay them something for their trouble.

I grew up in Murton and my parents are still there, and anybody that knows it well will be aware that just off the main street there is the cricket ground and a couple of colliery welfare football pitches just behind. With it being during the summer the posts were down and the grass hadn't been cut in ages, but we were getting desperate by this point and as it was one of the last places we could think of we fixed something up for them there.

Murton AFC were already on the field using it for pre season training though and they must have looked like Raggy Arsed Rovers, they all had different coloured tops on and were genuinely using jumpers for goalposts; some blokes were out walking their dogs too and there were even some whippets flying up and down one side of the pitch!

21

The scene was already looking ridiculous, and just then this immaculate team coach comes down the track. It was a top of the range bus, with the name proudly written on the front and the likes of Adrian Ilie coming off looking like stars. Then there was all of the club directors getting off looking like The Sopranos and these lads from Murton wouldn't get off the pitch would they?

I turned up and just felt so embarrassed. Pratty was there too and he tells the story really well now, but he must have wanted the ground to swallow him when it was happening. He still lived with his Mam and Dad at the time; they lived right next to the cricket ground so he was outside practising his batting when they turned up. To be fair to them though, they just took it as it was and starting training with the Murton lads, but I suppose they would considering the amount of bung they took just to turn up in the first place. Mind you, I think Murton is now to be twinned with Romania!

Things were hardly going to plan and I suppose it was not a surprise that I didn't even play a part in the game itself. I'd done my hammy in training the day before and because it was so close to the start of the proper season, our first in what was then called the Premiership, Reidy had to say to me "no, you're not playing". Still, it was a good evening and I was able to take my son Liam onto the Roker Park pitch, but we ended up losing 1-0.

Come the end of the night we had a presentation for the Steaua Bucharest players in one of the suites in the Main Stand. The mementoes we were handing out were made out of glass yet even before I got up to hand them out to people bits were falling off so you had all of these international footballers standing there with them in their hands and they were dropping to bits; I was getting them out of a cardboard box and they hadn't even been wrapped properly. I couldn't even bring myself to shake their hands properly, and I bet that these fellas must have thrown them straight in the bin as soon as they got the chance. At the end of the day I knew I had to give the Bucharest party something for coming over but I look back and honestly think they would have been better off even if we had given them something daft like a cigarette lighter.

The trophies carry on was just another example of corners being cut, and that side of things was a bit of a disaster. Having said that, it is rare that a footballer is given a testimonial these days so I still think myself lucky now to have had so many good nights and to have been able to meet as many supporters as I did, but it says it all that even the dinner at Rainton Meadows, successful as it was, ended up causing a domestic.

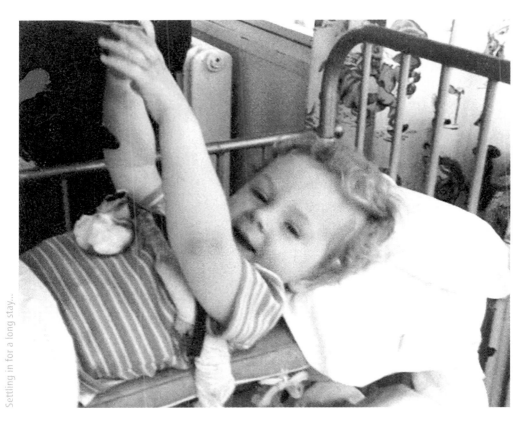

Settling in for a long stay...

CHAPTER THREE

He's from Murton; that's for certain

Question; Which Sunderland player broke his leg when they beat Leeds in the 1973 FA Cup Final?

Answer; Richard Ord.

Okay, so it's a bit of a trick question and I have to admit that I don't remember much about it; but it is a true story and my Mam remembers it vividly of course. I was at my Gran's watching the game on television with a football by my feet and when the final whistle went I jumped up in excitement and landed on the ball and fell awkwardly. There was a bloke that lived up the street that was a paramedic and he rushed down to see to me, and apparently on the way to hospital the roads were deserted because everybody was still inside watching the coverage. I was in hospital for 12 weeks whilst I recovered, but on the plus side when the players were back home they brought the trophy into the Children's Ward and I got on the local news with the Cup next to me.

Dad was at Wembley for the game and Mam reckons that when he rang home she didn't dare tell him what had happened as it would have spoiled his day. She'd had a ticket for the game too but had decided not to go, mainly because I had only just returned home after an even longer spell in hospital with a condition called Perthes Syndrome and had been trying to build my strength up.

The Perthes was a very difficult time for my family and I think my Mam and Gran were always very protective of me as a result; when I was older and was playing in the street you could always see them hovering. It was first spotted because as a toddler I would always walk so it was unusual for me to start asking for carries; the ball in my hip socket and one of my knee caps hadn't developed properly though so my leg flicked out at an angle and in the end I spent over a year in traction.

Perthes was very rare but in one sense I was fortunate; our doctor knew a lot about it and diagnosed it straight away. I was sent to Monkwearmouth Hospital just to be assessed and my parents came away not knowing what had hit them; I was put straight on a frame and they had to leave me in hospital. Even back then all I played with was a ball and Mam remembers the nurse allowing me to kick it around the ward, simply because she knew that I was about to be put on this frame and wouldn't be able to do anything like that for a long time.

For something so uncommon it was funny that one of the other children in there with me was also from the same village as me. We never moved from our frames whilst we were there, we even had to eat our food on them and the older children would swing towels over their heads to pass things from one another, so I tried to copy them. We would pass toy cars between ourselves and my parents would bring me a new one every day because that was all we could play with.

When I was moved to Grindon Hall, which at the time was where all the Sunderland players went when they were injured, Mam would have to take two buses every day just so she could come and sit with me. Dad would then follow her straight from work and in the end they had to buy their first car because it was taking so long getting there and back every day. Gran would come through too of course and apparently there was a time when we were all left outside for fresh air and ended up getting sun stroke so they played war with the staff!

When I finally got out I had to learn everything again, so the leg break just made things worse. Gran, who was one of the most important people in my life, spent a lot of time with me when I was back home and she was the head of the family really. Everybody went to her house and looked up to her, and she was always helping people. We always used to go for Sunday dinner at my Gran's when I was a child and they are fond memories despite the early health problems.

All the lads would go to the pub, whilst the kids would either play outside or be watching Shoot. The fire would be roaring away inside and Gran would always wear her pinny no matter what. She was set in her ways but very loving; it used to be embarrassing because it would always be 'our Richard this' or 'our Richard that' and whenever you would try and tell her not to upset the others she would say 'no, I'll tell it to their faces, you're my favourite!'.

Gran would properly spoil you; and the family was everything to her. I saw then that you need your family around you; I am very grounded and quite shy really, and it is probably because of the upbringing I had where I never wanted for anything, even when I was a teenager during the miners strikes. They had a big impact on County Durham; people were even having to go to the Welfare Hall just for something to eat, but again, Gran bailed us out so we were very lucky compared to others.

We used to nick off from school or go down at lunch time to watch the pickets; they were absolutely horrendous. 'The terrace' where we lived was on the main drag of shops; there were riots at the bottom of road during the strikes; cars were overturned, the pub was alight and a couple of mates that I speak to now got locked up so when I started playing football professionally I perhaps appreciated it even more than most and would try and repay my Gran and my Mam and Dad - not that they would accept much.

My parents and my Dad especially, are very quiet people too and only say something when it has to be said. Both of them had difficult upbringings so they made a point of trying to give my two sisters and me a good start, and they did it; so they and my Gran are my idols in that respect. I think they were courting for ten years whilst they saved up to buy their first house and it must have been a struggle because Dad was always getting thrown out by his father Dodi, so perhaps that is why they wanted to have things the way they did for us.

I would sometimes get called 'RJ' because Dad is also called Richard and my Mam's Dad was John; I'm the eldest and our Helen is a year younger than me. Kimberly came a little bit later and is nine years younger. We all lived at 42 Woods Terrace in Murton until I bought a house at the top of the village and to me Murton will always be home, although I was actually born in Little Thorpe which is a tiny village on the way to Easington Colliery. The maternity hospital closed down shortly after so I was one of the last people born there.

My Mam's family are called Walton and her mother died when she was two. Her Dad, who was called John Walton believe it or not, had actually just signed for Liverpool but had to come back and work down the pits because there was no money. They lived at the Waterworks, and Mam had to go and live with my Auntie Margaret who was very strict and old fashioned; I think there was a few of them all squeezed in the one house. Auntie Christine, who is not really related and lost her mother, was brought up in there too and I think children were required to be seen and not heard.

She has an older sister too called Marjorie, but she moved away when she got married because my Uncle Ron was in the RAF, and then her Dad remarried to an awful woman seemingly; I think at that point Mam even had to have a spell in Barnardo's. We would visit my Uncle and Aunt during the holidays and they moved back up here later, and I do also remember meeting her Dad, but I was only five or six at the time and I can picture him being a very big bloke, very smart, and he apparently liked the women from the stories that you hear.

I think I get my height from that side of the family. Mam is tall for a woman, she ran for the county and was school champion at pretty much everything; high jump, long jump, javelin, discus and the 100 metres; she was very fit. Dad is a little bit shorter, but he loves his sport too. He also had a tough childhood from what I have been told and he had to learn how to stand up for himself.

There's a really good photograph of his father, Dodi, with one of his greyhounds in the book released to commemorate Sunderland's 100th year in the Football League, and he and Gran were very well known in the area. Dodi would get up on stage and sing and perform around the clubs, but going from the stories I have heard he was allegedly a bit of a rogue and as I was kept away from the more negative side of things I only really have vague memories. When he got older and was in a Home I used to take my own bairns to see him but it was difficult to talk to him; although he was very close to my eldest Liam and he used to call him his 'little bugger' and hit him playfully with his walking stick. I loved him because he never did anything to me, but I know that my Dad hated him for how he treated Gran.

Dad was a proper pitman and is the best supporter I ever had. I call Mam a groupie sometimes because she has kept loads of old pictures and articles about me but Dad, he never missed a game throughout my time at school; he would even take shifts off or use his holidays and when I played cricket for the county he would take me all over the place. He used to work at Dawdon and I even remember one night when the car was knackered he biked from work all the way to Easington just so he could watch me play football. Another time, the car had packed in again so he biked from Dawdon to Peterlee in the middle of winter, watched me play, then biked back and did another shift; I couldn't believe it when I saw him on the touchline.

He never used to say a word though; he would never have a go if I did something wrong. I've done a lot of youth coaching since retiring from playing and you will see Dads screaming and jumping up and down on the touchline and it's wrong. I have children myself, my eldest Liam and twins Charlie and Jessica and both the boys have played football and cricket but I like to follow my Dad and will keep quiet unless they ask for advice; if they have done well you say so, but that's it. All three mean the world to me, but if you go overboard most kids will just go into their shell.

Dad was steady away at every sport he tried and back then he was mad on football and cricket. He started cricket quite late because I think he thought it was a game for toffs and grammar school kids, but once he got into it he really took to it. Back then different areas or pubs would have their own teams, there were a lot of good players in Murton but they couldn't be bothered to play seriously so they would play games of 'knock out' in the street. Dad was a left hand bat, right arm bowler and his team were called Diddy's Doddy Men, so through that he got asked to play for the cricket club and we would spend our summers down there; the place would be packed with all the players' families watching on.

It was at the club that I met my best mate Michael Pratt, it was right on his door step and I think he assumed the place was his growing up! His brother John was a year older than me and he was a good cricketer too, and like me Pratty was always there. It doesn't matter what troubles I have had, Michael has been there to look after me or cheer me up and we are similar in a lot of ways; his Dad Tommy was involved in local football and got recognised by Durham FA for his contribution as secretary of Murton, and just like me Pratty really loves football and cricket so we were always together. He has barely changed since then, he was just a cheeky little kid with blonde curly hair that would take the mick out of everybody, and he should have had a lot more slaps than he has had by now to be honest!

As young boys he came on his first holiday abroad with us; he insisted on getting the window seat and climbed over Mam, who hates flying anyway and then felt even worse. Mam loves him really though and always brings up the story of when we went to a restaurant for a meal one evening during the holiday; Pratty uses Pitmatic a lot when he talks and some local people find it hard to understand him, never mind those that don't speak English very well, so when the waiter came out and asked him how he liked his bacon he replied "bournt" and it still makes her smile now.

The cricket club was the hub of Murton, so I soon got heavily involved and my sister Kimberley played for a while too. Taking part in all of this sport was great, although whilst I think I was probably above average school wise I was always out playing either football or cricket and it meant I didn't revise enough; when I was about to leave I had passed my mock exams but in the six weeks between them and the real ones the cricket season started up and the football season was drawing to a close so I was out every night and barely looked at a text book.

I ended up with five 'O' Levels, but I could have got more if I am honest. I was never a trouble maker at school though, and I think the nearest I ever got to being in trouble was when I was hauled up to the front in assembly in junior school. There had been stories that I had formed some sort of gang, but it was not my style at all and I think that because I was the tallest in the school I stood out and people would just make stuff up.

Both my parents are animal lovers and somehow they had managed to afford a horse when I was a boy. They kept it in a field in Wembley, funnily enough, which is in Murton and Dad would go over every day to take care of it, and our Yorkshire Terrier was renowned on the terrace because basically it was an idiot. Mam would let it out and when people went past on their bike Nipper would chase after them; honestly it must have had more lives than a cat because it was always getting ran over by cars. People would knock on the door to hand him over and say 'Here Mrs Ord, he's nearly dead again' and yet it would always pull itself round.

I don't think their love of animals has rubbed off on me; I have had a few dogs, mainly for the kids, but they have always ended up going to live at my parents. When I was 11 or 12 Helen got a hamster, but it broke free from its cage and ran over my face when I was lying in bed and I was that scared that I slept downstairs on the sofa for six weeks until it did it again and I couldn't sleep at all! It's amazing how long it lasted before we found this hamster, and I have never been keen on animals since, but I do think Jess has got her love of animals from my side.

Even now, Mam and Dad have dogs and they take them out every day and I must be the only one that doesn't like animals. Kimberley's little boy has a white rat and has budgies flying about all over, and Helen shows her award winning whippets all over the country. Her husband Graeme is a Sunderland fanatic, and so is their eldest, but I think he goes berserk with all of these dogs, and yet when we were at the cricket club once watching a game a whippet came running across the pitch towards us and bit a chunk out of her leg; she still has the scar now but loves the breed.

Both my sisters had no option but to come and watch either Dad or myself playing, unless the weather was really bad and they would stay in with Mam. They have their own lives now and have moved out of the village - things are different to my Gran's era. Murton is not the same either; our old house is still there but the things like the sweet shop opposite have long gone. All the development happens toward Dalton Park and the retail estate; you are okay if you need a cheap pair of football boots for example but it doesn't do so much day to day stuff. Mam will go across and likes to think she is getting a bargain though, she will walk over and always comes back with something for me whether I want it or not; she'll ask 'do you like this?' and because I can't tell her no I must have about 20 jackets now from Marksy's that I'll never wear!

Whenever you go round to visit my parents now you can guarantee Dad will be watching some sport or other on the television; Mam hasn't got a say in the matter. He plays more golf now than anything else, but I don't think Mam is bothered because it gets him out of her hair for a bit. As well as the cricket he played as a full back for Murton Democratic Club on Saturday mornings; he was quite quick, although he hates it when I say he was nothing exceptional! Before he would go to Roker every other week too, and at one point he went to all the away games as well. He is a huge Sunderland fan and always talked about the time he took Mam to see Manchester United at Roker Park. It was the night of the crushing when the gates collapsed so she didn't even get into the ground, and Mam was that scared she didn't return until I was playing.

Dad was always there though, right at the back of the Roker End with his mates and he has told me that I'd wanted to go a lot sooner than I did but he thought I would be too young. The first time he did take me he built a little wooden seat with a patch of carpet on it for me to go on the barrier, and Roly Gregoire was making his debut. I was listening to my Dad and his mates, all big pitmen, and I was in awe of them. Gregoire made a mistake and one of them shouted 'ow man, you fanny' and they all started laughing, so I thought it must have been clever to say things like that and copied him the next time Gregoire did something; but a copper tapped me on the shoulder and said if he heard me do it again he would throw me out and Dad reckoned I looked like I was going to be sick!

That was my first taste of Roker Park; nine years later I would be making my second 'debut' and in the build up to kick off I probably felt just as ill.

Bright eyed and ready to go

CHAPTER FOUR

Schoolboy stuff

I was always a bit of a Mammy's boy, crying on my first day and all of that at Murton County Primary School because I didn't want to go in and what have you. I was very shy as a child too; Mam always says that the first time she ever heard me shout was on a football pitch, but on my second day at school somebody kicked a plastic ball over to me and I just controlled it and smacked it - there was a big shed at one side of the yard with a pole one side that we used for a goal and the ball flew into the top corner. All of the older lads were really impressed and sure enough I soon settled in.

At the time the school had a crack side and the pitch was across the way from the school so I used to go and watch them play in their sky blue strips quite a lot, and I got to know the older lads really well because everybody was tightly knit. Mr Nelson ran the side, he was a big bloke but very calm natured, and he was another one that loved his football. He had big swept back hair and he ended up being my teacher for two years as well as my football coach. I got trials for the side during my second year of junior school, and despite being so young I got in; one of my first games I was running up and down so hard trying to impress that I ended up getting a massive stitch and keeled over so Mam ran on, like they do.

Murton was renowned for having good teams and the side that I had been watching had John Ord in it, who was a distant relative and ended up on Newcastle's books. Paul Kitson was a year younger than me and he too played for the team when he was much younger than the rest of the boys. Paul was centre forward even back then and he broke every record going, I was in centre midfield in those days though and I tried to base myself on Glen Hoddle and Johan Cruyff so I was basically his quarter back putting it through for him, although I would try and score the odd one myself!

School was about 300 yards up the road from home so at dinner time I would race back, hoy my Sunderland strip on and just go in the street kicking my ball. I would get told off by people because they had their lines of washing out, and when Mam and Dad told me to come in for my dinner I would always ask for five more minutes! Woods Terrace was a typical old street a bit like you saw in the film Billy Elliott, but it was shaped in a T junction. The coal bunker was at an angle and I didn't realise it at the time but all I was doing was playing the ball off one wall, opening myself out to play it off the bunker then turning again to play it off my wall, which is exactly the type of skill I try and drum into kids now when I am coaching. If you play in midfield the best thing you can do is to open yourself out, and I was doing it for hours and hours without giving it a second thought.

That street was always full of kids; they were older than me mainly so they brought me on, always knocking on the door and asking 'is he allowed out Mrs Ord'. Two lads especially; Ian and Barry Blyth, who lived on the corner, would always say something like 'ha'way, you need to practise on your right foot' or that I should do this or that. Even in the dark nights we would play under the street lights and I used to be gutted because being the youngest I would get called in first and all the others would take the water! On the odd occasion my parents might let me stop out a bit later they would get a bag of chips for us to share, and memories like that mean a lot even now; my childhood was idyllic and I bet loads of other kids wish they could have had that too.

At the top of the street lived old Mrs Graham and bless her, her house would always be where the 'goal' was so her windows always seemed to be getting smashed.

She would often get upset to be honest but now I can see where she was coming from because it was constant - if it wasn't football it would be cricket and all the parents would forever have to be organising whip rounds to get the glass replaced.

After the County I moved up to Easington Comprehensive and I loved it, it was a good school. You spent three years in the buildings next to the Colliery and the final two at the upper buildings in the village. That was the time to really get your head down and concentrate, but I was just all about sport. Mickey Shepherd, who was from Seaham, was the PE teacher and we had trials for the school football team and he couldn't make his mind up as to who should play. He asked all of the lads to vote, but of course there was only two schools from Murton feeding into the comp and three from Easington, so all of the lads were sticking their hands up for their mates and I didn't get picked!

I honestly was distraught because I was desperate to keep playing and I think some of the Murton parents had a few words somewhere along the line because suddenly there was another trial and not only was I put in the team, but Mr Shepherd told me I was going to be captain. It was all a bit odd; I don't know how you can go from not being in the side one day to being named the captain the next, but again we had a great side. We won the County Cup in consecutive seasons whilst I was playing for the school and most of the team played for the East Durham district side too, including me.

Our centre forward was Gavin Houghton; he was very quick and was bigger and stronger than the rest so we could knock the ball through for him all of the time. Of that side, John Graham went to Ipswich Town and the goalkeeper Paul O'Connor was at Hartlepool United before moving over to Hong Kong to play. I was closest to a lad called Ray Sillito and I ended up being very good mates with him, I used to spend a lot of time through at Easington at his house at this stage.

There were different representative teams you could get selected for, school, district, county and then England schoolboys but I didn't even get as close as a trial for England at this stage; I was probably one of the better players in the district but that was about it. I wasn't even first choice for the county side because Gary Breeds played in the same position as me. Breedsy was frightening then, the best player I had seen then by a distance and he ended up at Sunderland with me after school.

Neil Maddison was in the county set up too, and we would be alternated alongside Breedsy in the centre of midfield. Neil went to Southampton with Alan Shearer because the club had an academy based up here in the north east and he played in the top flight for a long time. Ray was going through to Gateshead to work with the Southampton coaches as well at this point too.

I loved Glen Hoddle and he, Kevin Keegan and Gary Rowell were my favourites and in later years I was fortunate enough to meet them all at different points. As a player myself though I was never the most mobile so I just used to try and get the ball and ping it but I used to think of myself as a bit of a keeper as well, just through playing in the street. When you are against the older lads it was always the old 'you are the youngest, get in goal' but it didn't do me much harm because we were down playing against South Yorkshire in some national competition and neither of our goalkeepers were available so I was able to volunteer to go in.

I think one of the lads had missed the coach and the other fell ill on the journey I wasn't bothered by the idea of going in though and it might have been my turn to sit out for Maddison anyway so I gave it a go and honestly, I was unbelievable! It was surreal, I seemed to be making save after save and was thinking to myself 'how am I doing this' but with about five minutes to go I took a goal kick and ruptured my groin. I think it was probably through flinging myself all over making these saves so I was sitting on a stretcher when this bloke came into the changing rooms and said "aright son", but because I was in so much agony I was a bit rude and snapped "no, not really". He tried again though and told me he was a scout for Sheffield Wednesday and wanted to know if I would sign for them as a goalkeeper; my first game in sticks and he would have signed me, I thought it was a wind up.

I had to tell him the situation and he couldn't believe it. It shows that sometimes you have to be in the right place at the right time to get into football, although I would have been found out soon enough. I did always think however that had I been needed in an emergency I would have gone in goal for the first team, and would sometimes mess about in training and ask the lads to hit a few shots at me, but in truth I was always going to be an outfield player.

I was confident, but not arrogant, on the pitch and even when I was taken out of the comfort zone of being with my mates in the school team I could still produce the same performances. Perhaps I could have afforded to be more arrogant in some respects, as that often is what sets the top players apart, but back then I was never playing for any reason other than the fact I enjoyed it and seemed to be quite good. I didn't go around thinking I was going to do this in the game or I was going do that, and it was only when Middlesbrough offered me a trial that the idea of being a professional genuinely came into my head.

A scout had approached my Dad during a game and had asked me to play in a game at Ayresome Park. This guy had brought players like Colin Cooper and Gary Pallister into the club and he was highly thought of, and I did enough in the match to be asked back so they could take a further look at me. Before that though I had an important match for the school at Easington Colliery Welfare Club and I was told I could play, which proved to be massive for me.

We were in the semi final of the County Cup against Pelton Roseberry. It was a bit of a needle match because we seemed to get drawn against them every year and I gave the best performance I had for my school; I was passing the ball here there and everywhere and scored a couple of beauties out on this massive pitch. I came off feeling pretty pleased with myself anyway but Dad came over and told me George Herd had been there; I hadn't even heard of him but he had been one of my Dad's favourites and within a week or two Sunderland asked to sign me. Middlesbrough were still on my case though but Dad just said "no arguments, you are signing for Sunderland!"

All of the school games were played on Saturday mornings, so I never missed a Sunderland home game at this point anyway and it was not as if Dad had needed to make my mind up for me. I used to go over with a lad called David Wilson, who lived at the top of the terrace and was two years older than me. We'd got to know each other through playing football out in the street and even now I think he still goes to a lot of Sunderland's matches. Just like my Dad we would always go towards the back of the Roker End before it was cut in size for safety reasons, and from there I remember seeing John Hawley score an absolute stunner against Arsenal. It must be the best goal I have ever seen, and people still talk about it today. David and I watched it again on television but it was even better live.

I'll always remember signing the Associate Schoolboy forms with my Dad, George and the secretary at Roker Park. The date was 16 March 1984, I think the room we used was the manager's office and Paul Bracewell stuck his head round the door and shook my hand; this was during his first spell here when Alan Durban had a really good young side. Youth football was totally different to how it is now, there was a lot less involvement with the clubs and it was more a case of them just keeping tabs on you really before signing you as an apprentice - you didn't even play games for them at weekends, you just played for your school, representative or junior sides and as a lad I also managed to squeeze in playing for Wheatley Hill Juniors in the Teesside Alliance League and Murton Juniors in the Hetton Youth League.

With Sunderland all we used to do was go once a week to the Northumbrian Centre in Washington, and of course Dad would try and change his shifts so he could take me. George would train us, and he was brilliant, he was always standing with Dad at games and they would talk about football for hours. I used to think his sessions were great because he would do a lot of new things; he had been to Dubai and Kuwait a lot and would bring new ideas back.

Sunderland would make you come in over the holidays too and you got involved with the apprentices and the jobs they did. In those days they were told to do everything; they would have two pros each that they were responsible for and they would have to sort kit and clean their boots. Clubs are not allowed to make them do that anymore, but for us it was good practise for when we got taken on.

There were question marks over whether I would get signed as a full time apprentice, as I'd been told verbally that I was going to get one but you needed a letter of confirmation and I was waiting and waiting. I had a falling out with my Dad over it because he sat me down and said "look son, it doesn't look like its going to happen so you are going to have to thinking about college or something like that" and I went berserk, I think I sat outside in the car for hours crying.

What I didn't realise at the time was that he was just looking out for me, but I still had belief in my ability and when he saw how much it meant I think he went to the club and asked around on my behalf. Jim Morrow was Youth Development Officer and had worked with England before Lawrie McMenemy got him in, George had left by this point and Jim was being a bit funny with me, I felt he was blanking me and all of that. It was probably because I was George's signing and not his, so I think Dad approached Chris McMenemy, who was Lawrie's son and had also just arrived at the club, and he told him not to worry.

Chris took a few training sessions with me and we had a final trial on the site where the Academy of Light is now. He came up to me afterwards and told me I had done well and within a couple of days the letter was there, so I think Chris did push my case in the end. It sounds like a cliché but you've got to want it more than anything; I wasn't the best player at school or county but I just wanted it that much and I think that's what got me through, the want of playing for Sunderland. It would have killed my Dad to have said he didn't think it would happen, he doesn't drink much but when the letter arrived he went out that night and got bladdered; he was over the moon.

What perhaps makes the football progress so pleasing was the fact that I always felt I was better at cricket at that stage. With my Dad playing for Murton and the family always there watching I soon wanted to get involved as a young boy and so he spoke to a bloke called Alan Graham on my behalf. This guy was basically 'Mr Murton Cricket Club' and he lived for cricket. He was a real gentleman and was very good with the children when they were around the club; he gave me some practise equipment and told me he would help me as much as I wanted.

I took to it quickly and my first game for the Under 15s was when I was only seven! I was surrounded by all of these giants, but Alan had taught me all of the correct basics, so I felt comfortable. I hit the first ball I faced and it went for four, and I still remember it because everybody was cheering me on. Next delivery though, and this older lad shouted me through for a run and I got ran out; I was in tears!

There weren't any younger age groups at the time so I would often field for the Under 15s after that and I was always there; if I wasn't practising or playing I would do the scoring for the first team. The club was part of the community, there would be quiz nights at the club and we would go on coaches to away games and stop over at places. I loved cricket, I still do, and during the summer holidays I would happily sit in front of the television for five days to watch the Test matches on the BBC, I would see every single ball of every single over.

I helped start up the first cricket team the comp had and because I was one of the few lads that was already playing we shared some of my gear out and got the rest through hand outs from parents or people at Murton Cricket Club. We were actually a good team though and that first year we won the County Cup, which was unheard of for a state school. We played at the lower school on an artificial pitch and when Durham School turned up for the semi final and saw half of us in plimsolls that were meant to be for gym class they began laughing and telling us they would turn us over, but we sent them away with their tails between their legs and then beat Yoden Hall in the final.

Through playing for Murton's Under 15s I got picked for Durham at Under 13s, even though I was only 11 by this point. I was asked to captain the side in my second year, which again was unheard of for a lad from one of the collieries. Cricket has always had that public school background but I always got on with the lads from the county side despite the different backgrounds; which were summed up once when Matty Roseberry, whose son Andrew was in the team with me, came to pick me up in a big Mercedes and lots of people from the street came out just to look at his car.

As captain we went down to Old Trafford to play, but the day before we set off I broke my bat. It was a Gray Nicholls Power Spot and I'd had it forever, so whilst everybody was offering me one to borrow the only one I felt comfortable with was wrapped up in tape, it was a right state. Walking to the crease at Old Trafford as a 14 year old was a great experience, but the pitch was much faster than I was used to and I fell to pieces. I was used to playing quite puddingy wickets on local club pitches so the ball was flying through over my head and all of the Lancashire lads were taking the mick out of me and my bat, they must have thought I was a right chancer. I was in for about an hour and a half and I only got 12; I couldn't hit the ball but at least I can say I played there.

I made my debut for the Murton first team the same season, opening the batting when the Vaux Coast League was still a really good standard. The league had overseas players and all of that; I was up against real big men. My second game was against South Hetton, who had a pro called Zach Kahn, just when helmets were being introduced. You could decide whether you wore one or not, but I hated them and of course got hit straight in the face by Kahn's second delivery. At first he was trying to make sure I was okay and I started crying like a right one, but Dad ran on with a helmet and I just got angry, I was walking down the wicket and whacking the ball back over him and all sorts. All that did was wind him up and he nearly had me by the throat at one point - I got 40 odd in the end, which wasn't a bad effort after being so dazed, and I continued to play for the firsts and then the Coast League Select side until the football took over.

You only got picked up for cricket when you were 16 and leaving school really, I was playing in some final against Hetton Lyons and I got sixty odd so this bloke approached me afterwards and wanted me to go on trial at Northamptonshire. Northants had been sniffing for a while but it was too far down the line and I had already made the decision and signed for Sunderland; you couldn't mix the two and when they came calling that was it for me.

The cricket club has gone backwards now. I don't go down much anymore because there isn't that community interest and it is a shame, but they do have a new club house these days; the old one had to be knocked down because they had a few problems with Bats, which was ironic I suppose. As a kid though you couldn't tear me away, I had a snooker table in the middle of the dining room for a while and there was always cricket gear or sports kit hanging up to dry in there. If games were called off the lads would come round to play snooker; Mam must have been sick with it all!

That was it for fun and games though, I had signed for Sunderland as a full time apprentice and was moving out; the real work was about to begin.

I may not be smiling much, but after settling in I loved being a trainee

CHAPTER FIVE

Roker Rookie

My Youth Training Scheme at Sunderland started for the 1986-87 season whilst Lawrie McMenemy was manager. One of the things he introduced at the club was a hostel for the YTS players and given the close knit family I grew up in I suppose it was little wonder that I missed home in the early days of my time there.

We were based on the sea front in Roker in one of those big town houses, but looking back the building was quite stark. The first night I arrived was a very daunting experience; I know it was only a few miles away from home but being dropped off was like being a little school boy all over again. I'd gone from seeing these lads in training once a week and perhaps a bit more during the summer to actually living with them and it felt like a different world.

I know it sounds stupid but I felt homesick straight away. I had been wrapped up in cotton wool by Mam and Dad I suppose so it was a completely new environment for me and at first I was that unhappy that Dad had to come over, bring me back home to Murton for an hour and then drive me over again until I was settled. It wasn't that I didn't want to be at the club or anything like that, but I soon pulled round and was getting stuck in; all the other lads were in the same boat after all.

I was right at the top of the building and I got put in with a lad called Johnny Hepple. He was from a really rough area of Middlesbrough and was playing Northern League football for South Bank since he was 15. Jim Morrow went down to look at him and decided to sign him straight away, but if you look at photos from then he had tattoos even when he was 16 year old kid and he was obviously a bit of a character. He would never stop talking and was as brave as a lion on the pitch but I don't think he had any stability in his life and it held him back.

He was Jim's favourite and would be allowed to go home, so obviously he would go out on the drink and would come back with love bites on his neck every Monday morning. I think that was why Jim tried to be a fatherly figure, but as soon as he was away from the club that would be it. He did sign a pro contract at Sunderland but never made the first team, and a couple of years ago Gary Owers told me that he had died suddenly. He felt alone I think, and it was a real shame he didn't get to show what he could do.

Gary Breeds of course was another one of the golden boys, but the favourable treatment did him no good either I reckon because he didn't become the player he could have done either. He was the only one that avoided moving into the hostel; he only lived round the corner in Redby but some of the lads felt it was more to do with Sunderland bending over backwards to sign him than anything else. He was an unbelievable player and clubs up and down the country wanted him, so we heard all sorts of rumours about what he had been given to get him to the club and it rubbed some of the others up the wrong way. I was naive enough to think everybody was clean cut, but really he would get away with all sorts at times and when we were going back to the hostel he'd be out with his mates giving it the big shot.

It was two to a room in the hostel. The lads all got on great and it was always fun and games; although Barry Richardson and Jarred Suddick were in a room together and always thought they were the pin up boys and so they got a bit of stick; when they used to go out they would put make up on their faces to cover their spots and all of that! Those two were from Whitley Bay and most of us were from the North East, Nicky Jimson was a hard solid left back from Middlesbrough for example and he was in a room with Gary Owers who lived in Washington and had been from

Birtley originally. Paul McKenzie was Scottish so he was from a little further afield though, and so was Sean Wharton, who was from Wales. Sean was a lovely lad; he played once for the first team but never recovered when he did a cruciate, although I think Gary still talks to him now. Mitchell Wellens was another member of the group, he was from Sunderland and although he got released he has still made himself a good career out of the sport; he calls himself 'Mr Football' and goes around the schools running coaching sessions.

Downstairs there was a pool room and a sitting room with a television, although we weren't allowed in the kitchen. The three women that ran it were called Margaret, Susan and Judith I think, they were sisters and were never off diets and of course when you get a group of young lads together you are bound to get shenanigans and wind ups so they must have had a job trying to look after all of us. It seemed that their fridge was always loaded and ours never had anything in, but you always got your three square meals a day. You would have to order your bacon and eggs the evening before otherwise it would be toast and cereal and after breakfast we would walk through Roker Park to the football ground to train before coming back for a light soup and sarnies lunch. Our main meal would then be at about six o'clock; the food wasn't great and we would always be taking the water, yet we'd all look forward to Friday because it was steak night. It doesn't sound much to get excited about now, and it probably wasn't that special at the time but to us it was a treat.

Most of the lads would go out on the town and there was a bit of pressure on me to follow. Gary Owers is my best mate in football, he has been ever since we met in the hostel, and he would like a night out but at time it didn't appeal to me; I was still shy in different surroundings then. I kept putting it off and making excuses but come Christmas time I knew I would have to sooner or later. I was back home over the holiday period but missed the bus from Murton, so had to walk to Cold Hesledon to get another one and half way there I just asked myself why I was bothering and turned back and went home. I got hammered from the lads for that when we were all back at the hostel, but I still didn't want to go afterwards and would instead listen to the lads creeping up the stairs every after Wednesday night, because that was the night to be seen, trying not to get caught.

Lawrie had brought his assistant Lew Chatterley and his staff to the club; if my memory is correct the old guard that had been with the club for years were peddled, and it seemed to me as if all of a sudden new staff were turning up in posh cars and all of this. Even Lew's boy moved up and got an apprenticeship, but whilst he was a nice kid I never felt he was going to make the grade. Chris McMenemy though was actually a great coach; he was talented and would join in during training and it was obvious that he had played a bit himself. He was very much a grounded person and he actually moved into the top end of Murton so would give me a lift on occasions. He took me under his wing a bit and I think it is fair to say that he liked me as an individual and as a player, so he looked after me a bit.

You would have to be at Roker Park for nine o'clock to train. It seemed that every day you were being asked to take part in a practise match against the first team because they were struggling so much for form and all Lawrie would do would sit up in the Main Stand executive boxes and watch. The first team had the likes of Eric Gates and honestly, it was embarrassing; we were just kids and they still couldn't beat us; we were all scratching our heads and thinking 'bloody hell' to ourselves.

It was to get even worse though; Lawrie then had them playing shadow football instead so that they could work on their shape, but the players were going through the motions really; big Iain Hesford threw the ball out but because Frankie Gray's first touch wasn't the best he played it back, and wouldn't you know it; the ball hit a bobble and went over Hessy's foot and into the net - they were getting beaten off nobody now! Gatesy loves to tell that story, but at the time it was terrible.

After that the YTS lads would sometimes have to run through to Whitburn and would then have our own training session. We would then get the bus back and have lunch before coming back for more training or to do chores, like getting things ready for the next day's training. My job was to look after the away team dressing room at Roker Park and at about five o'clock Chris would come and check up on you; he would run his finger along the top of the cupboards and that, and if he found any dust anywhere all the lads would have to stay back or be sent out on another run. Academy players are not required to do anything like that now, but you learned to respect things and I loved it personally; it was a dream for me to just to be going behind the scenes, it really was brilliant.

If the first team had a home game we would be expected to attend, and sometimes you would have to be there earlier, from 8 o'clock or so in the morning, and not get back to the hostel until 11 at night, but of course I didn't mind one bit because I got to see the match. We were given our two pros that we each had to look after; and there would be hell on if you hadn't prepared their stuff correctly for them.

Davey Corner and Paul Lemon were my two; Jackie Lemon was good to me but Davey was a right so and so. We get on great now, but at the time he would always be winding me up and at Christmas when all the lads were looking forward to getting a little bonus from their pros I ended up getting nowt off him!

The chores took up a lot of our time but we had our own games in the Northern Intermediate League to think about as well, although in the early stages of the season I wasn't getting into the team. When I got there, there was an overload of midfield players and at that time that was how I thought of myself, but because there was a shortage of defenders at reserve and youth level Chris pulled me and said he wanted to give me a go at centre half, and of course I said I would play anywhere. The next match was against Leeds United and Chris told me the night before that I would be playing, so I was going to make my debut in a position I had never really played in. Being as I am, I felt worried immediately and couldn't rest; but Hep kept telling me just to get to sleep. He was one of those that never worried about anything so was the exact opposite of me in that respect, but he was great in that situation and he managed to settle me right down.

We used to play our home games at the Northumbria Centre and it was a big pitch. Just like the first team we hadn't won a game either but it was a bright sunny October day and we beat them 3-1. We absolutely battered them in truth and I didn't feel out of place at the back so just kicked on from there. We thumped Lincoln 6-1 the following week in a run of four home games on the trot where we were unbeaten. I was an ever present at centre half for the rest of the season and whilst I wasn't the quickest I found I could read things and get into the correct positions and with me having played so much in midfield I was decent on the ball.

Before my time I think youth football was just about 'win win win' and our league was full of big, strong teams. Basically, it was long ball stuff but Chris was quite different; training was always with the ball at our feet and he would encourage us to pass round teams. Chris saw beyond results in some ways, but we did pick up a few good victories along the way when everything clicked; we won 6-0 away at Grimsby late on in the season and beat Newcastle at home, which was a bit of a battle even at that level. We won 4-1 down at Middlesbrough too, and in the main playing in defence seemed to be coming quite naturally to me. Chris said that he didn't really need to coach me and started calling me the 'new Mark Wright' having seen him brought through at Southampton, so that was a boost and made me feel even more at ease.

The FA brought through a pack that Chris had to carry out so he would sit us down and talk us through it. It required us to work on different areas like your weaker foot, stamina and now I was a defender, heading. Chris would set aside time where you could go away with a mate and work on the drills, and we also had to spend Thursday afternoons in college on a leisure course, where the idea was that we would all get a qualification. Clubs do this type of thing all the time now but it was a new system then and came in at the right time for me.

I was only 5ft 10, but I went through a few growth spurts and I was very dedicated at the time. I made sure that I never put a foot wrong; I was there whenever I was needed because I loved it, being in the team and being around the club, and wanted more. It was a case of being in the right place at the right time and there is always an element of luck in it with regards to the coaches liking you as a player and you avoiding injuries. I was already starting to get a lot of soft tissue injuries and obviously the medical side of things wasn't as tight as it is now, but I was always able to manage and get through games.

When I look back I was getting cramps and it was through growing; I don't think I stopped properly until I was 25, and that wasn't until then that I really felt comfortable and was at my strongest. I must have been doing something right though still, because I actually got a call up for the reserve team after having only played about 20 games in the Northern Intermediate side and made my debut at that level in the March, which was another big moment for me. The match was against Coventry City at Roker and ironically enough I played alongside one of my pros Davey in the middle of defence, and although the step up was noticeable I came off thinking I had given a decent account of myself. Sean Wharton was playing too and scored the only goal of the game so the night couldn't have gone much better.

I got four more starts before the end of the season and was on the bench a couple of times so got to experience Old Trafford, Goodison Park and Villa Park; not bad for somebody that couldn't get in the youth side at the start of the season! The club was in Division One of the Central League so we were playing at these famous grounds up against teams that included players with top flight football under their belts in many cases and that brought me on no end. People in my own team like Davey benefitted me too, not to mention Alan Kennedy.

Less than one year ago I was playing in school tournaments and whatever and now I was alongside a fella that had played for England and won the European Cup twice.

Alan was perhaps past his best when he came to Sunderland, you could say that about a lot of senior teams then, but you are bound to learn from being around people like that. I'd actually broken his leg during one of those training games Lawrie had us doing and then suddenly he turned up just before we were due to kick off against Sheffield United reserves having made his own way down.

He was building his fitness back up but hadn't been scheduled to play in the game, so it showed a bit of keenness to get back after what had originally been a nothing challenge to pick up the injury. It happened when the pitch was very wet and we'd both slid in for the ball in front of the dug outs and collided. He just got up and ran off, so minimal it seemed at first, but his leg didn't look quite right so he went and drove himself to hospital only to be told he'd fractured his leg!

There was no problem between us as he knew it was a freak incident and he was a funny bloke a lot of the time even though all around him the club was at its lowest ebb. It was getting to the point where Lawrie had to go; I knew a lot of fans thought he was a disgrace really and that he fleeced the club. It upset a few people how he gave jobs to his friends and family, although that is no disrespect to Chris because I liked him and felt he was there on merit. I felt though that Lawrie didn't put the effort in that was needed and thought he could buy a load of older pros and leave it to them. He tried to replicate what he did when he had been at Southampton, but things don't always work out like that twice and there was no 'Plan B'.

If I said we saw Lawrie two or three times to actually talk to that would be pushing it, I saw him once in a corridor at Roker and he patted me on the head and said 'alright Richard' like I was a little lad and yet I must have been his blue eyed boy for some reason because me and Gary were the only ones he would trust with washing his prized BMW. Every Friday afternoon we would be there outside the Main Stand cleaning this car and then when he was moving house he also gave us the job of shifting some of his gear. The order never came direct from him though, all you would see was this big figure in the executive boxes passing messages to people when he wanted things doing.

It hardly seemed as if I had been there for two minutes before the season was up and yet me and Gary were told we would both be getting professional contracts in the summer, it was unreal. Gary was a year older and had already progressed to the fringes of the first team and we even heard a rumour that Portsmouth, who were promoted to the top flight that season, had put a joint bid in for us so that might have forced the club's hand. I was hardly going to start asking how and why though and just wanted it done before anybody changed their mind.

Given how much I struggled at the start of the season I dread to think how I would have coped with a move to the other end of the country anyway, and I was never going to turn down a three year contract at Sunderland once I knew that was on the cards. I think Lawrie was still in his last days at the club and maybe he had been paying more attention than we realised, but for a first year trainee to be signed up was unheard of. I had been on £17.50 a week I think it was and was due to be going up to £25 in my second year as a YTS player, but instead I ended up on £75 and was moving back to Mam and Dad's so it was a double bonus.

Agents weren't as involved then so I did as I was told, not that I wanted to argue anyway. I think the deal went from £75 to £100 in the second year and then £125 in the third and you could say I was more than happy with that. Bob Stokoe had replaced Lawrie when he eventually flitted off but didn't have enough time to save the club from relegation and it meant I would be starting my career as a professional footballer in Division Three. My first year at Sunderland had been a whirlwind, yet the second soon proved even better; not just for me but thankfully for the club also.

The 'baby faced Murton teenager'

CHAPTER SIX

Teenage Kicks

There were a lot of changes behind the scenes during my year as an apprentice. Tom Cowie had been replaced as Chairman by Bob Murray, who after turning to Bob Stokoe then brought in Denis Smith and Viv Busby over the summer from York City. It was a new start for everybody and I think Bob must have told Smithy about me because he was giving me a shot even though he wouldn't have seen anything of me.

I was a year ahead of schedule and was in the first team changing room come the beginning of pre season, which meant I was now the one getting his boots cleaned and kit sorted! It was all a bit surreal really, but the YTS lads were alright with me and I didn't see any jealousy that I recall. As a 17 year old kid working with the first team squad I was keen to give it everything I had, but Smithy was trying to pick up a club that was in the third division for the first time in its history so perhaps having people like me and Gary about was a good thing to inject some energy.

47

I came on for the second half of a pre season warm up at Gretna and I remember getting the ball and looking up for Eric Gates or one of the other senior lads but none of them came short so I put the ball in the corner for them to chase instead and had a bit of a go at them afterwards. They were looking at me as if to say 'who do you think you are' but I'd done it without really thinking and expected to get a telling from Denis at the end, yet he went the other way and stuck up for me; he knew I was in the right and had done the correct thing in the first place so he made sure he praised me in front of the rest of the team.

After getting through pre season I was given a couple more games in the reserve team, which I had expected would be the case to be honest. There had been mutterings around the place that Smithy was about to give me a debut, but he left it a while because in Division Three you had people like big Joe Jordan at Bristol City who were way more physical and more experienced than I had come up against and I think he was worried I would be battered. At the end of October though I played at Roker in a 3-0 win against Blackpool for the reserves and then a week later it came, my first team debut for Sunderland AFC.

I should have only been in my second year as an apprentice really and had only started ten reserve team games in total and yet I was called into Smithy's office after training and told I was going to start against Southend United the following evening. I didn't know how to take it, I was buzzing about it of course, but the news meant another restless night. Come the day of the game we had light training on the morning before I went home and tried to get a bit of kip, but again it just didn't happen because my mind was still racing.

The Sunderland Echo made a big thing about me starting and Geoff Storey referred to me as the "baby faced Murton teenager" and all of that. Once that was printed Mam's phone didn't stop ringing with everybody asking for tickets; people from school, people from the cricket club, family, there were over 100 people I knew planning to be there and I think somebody even put a mini bus on from Murton so it was even more nerve-wracking now, thinking that I didn't want to let anybody down. When Denis came in to do his final pep talk I was still in the toilets, I felt that nervous; it was like watching Roly Gregoire all over again. It was Owersy that had to come in and put me right, he had already been a brotherly figure to me in some ways with him that bit older and having made his own debut in the first game of the season was approaching 20 appearances, so he knew the score.

Night games were always special at Roker Park, even at that level, and I know it is a cliché, but it honestly was a dream come true as I walked out onto the pitch on 3rd November 1987 to make my debut. There had been a lot of hard work getting to this stage but it was actually happening, although I was more proud for my Mam and Dad than myself I think and of course they had made sure they were there with my sisters - along with virtually everybody else from the village it seemed. As for the game itself, the dream was getting better; we won 7-0 and it was our biggest victory in over 31 years. Gatesy scored four, Paul Atkinson got two and Marco Gabbiadini, who was fast becoming a crowd favourite after arriving just into the season, got another for his tally.

Paul played for England at youth levels and he had it all really, he was lightning fast but he liked a burger and he liked a pint otherwise he would have featured more; plain and simple. He then got a bad injury and everything went down hill from there for him, but he was always a nice bloke and I still like to talk to him now; and it pays to do so sometimes. He knew a fella that was starting up a sports bar in Sunderland called 'My Legends' and he asked me, Atky and Gordon Armstrong to come down for the opening night in 2007. We had our taxis paid for, were given as much to drink as we wanted and were even paid £100 each for the privilege! It was the easiest money I've ever made, but were it not for that debut who knows if I would have made a career for myself and been remembered nearly 20 years later.

Southend had a chance after about 20 seconds but other than that we bossed it. I had one dodgy moment in the game when the ball came across the box and I tried to take a touch, like I normally did, but it was a bad one and I had to react quickly to clear the ball. I got away with it though, so it was the only time during the match itself where my heart jumped and other than that I felt as if I did really well; I was up against two forwards called Martin Robinson and Roy McDonough, who was quite strong and was known to have a bit of a short fuse, but I still won every header and when I got possession I kept it. I even had a hand in our first two goals; I won the ball for our first and started the move and then just before half time I put a pass through their defence for Atky to finish, so not bad going for somebody that had only started my YTS 18 months earlier.

I came off after about 70 minutes and another County Durham lad called Micky Heathcote came on for his debut as my substitute, but were it not for cramp I would have perhaps stayed on for the full 90. I'd never really had it before but obviously everything had got to me so when I went up for a header from an attacking corner in front of the Fulwell End I felt this pain and ended up having to be stretchered off right round the running track; I was applauded by everybody though and that was great - it made up for having to come off.

Everybody was on a high in the changing room afterwards, which you would expect after winning so well and it was great to be around and feel I had played my part. After a fairly mixed start this was our eighth win in nine games and I think as a side we had got to grips with the division. We were a big fish in a little pond in some ways, there had been over 15,000 in the crowd that night and I doubt many other clubs could match that, and the class of some of the players was telling. We didn't lose another league game until the back end of February and we had showed that night that we had the best squad in the division.

When you look at the team that played against Southend there was a great blend; Gary was breaking through and Gabbers was flying just as his 'G-Force' partnership with Gatesy was kicking in. There were a few older heads too that helped me through it all and put an arm round me like Frankie Gray, and even Gatesy helped out in his own way. Frankie was at left back and he oozed confidence and composure, and you just had to look at him and it would settle you down. Iain Hesford had loads of experience and talked me through the game and of course being alongside John MacPhail in the centre of defence was a big plus.

Monty was a great player and I don't think people always realised it. He wasn't the quickest, but he was the best I ever saw at reading it and Denis would often tell me 'you just watch him, and you will learn loads', and I did to be fair. He was another calming influence, which you need on occasions like your debut, and he was excellent at getting in front of the striker when their goalkeeper would clear it, which meant that the centre forward would have to try and get back but would end up giving away the foul.

I was going out with Nicola Stevens, a Ryhope girl, and all of her family were there too so after the game we all went to her parents' house for a bit of a celebration. It was early to bed for me though and back for training the next day, all very normal, all very matter of fact and that was it, done and dusted. I was now a first teamer and I was expected to take it in my stride. The Echo referred to it as an "encouraging debut" and I stayed in the team for a couple of games after that and went from nothing to playing three first team games at Roker Park in the space of 11 days.

We only managed a draw against Grimsby Town on the Saturday after piling the pressure on them and the following week I played in the FA Cup against Darlington.

I deserved my place I felt, but was certainly helped by the injury crisis at the club; Gary Bennett and Davy Corner were both injured and Frankie had just come back in for Reuben Agboola, who was also out, yet he too took a knock against Southend and even poor Micky Heathcote had to get stretched off on his debut as well after we had used our substitutes.

My first away game was at Chesterfield, where we took a massive following as always. They seemed to have a large pitch and I still wasn't physically there, but we were getting the ball down and passing it and that was my game all over really so I fitted in perfectly and felt I was playing well. Denis even came out in the papers talking me up and I think it was Frank Johnson that wrote a piece about Sunderland 'finding the new Charlie Hurley'; I did think it was a little bit over the top because when people read something like that they start expecting you to be out of this world but in the main fans recognised that I was learning my way so wasn't under too much pressure.

I roomed with George Burley for the trip to Chesterfield and as I was new to it all I sat at the front of the team bus wondering what would go on. We got to the hotel and before we went down for our meal George got this little bag out and put a set of ironed pyjamas on the bottom of his bed, making sure he didn't crease them, and at this point I felt right out of place because I was just planning on sleeping in the buff! We then had dinner and all of the lads started cracking on, but George told me we had to go up to our room and I was forced to leave the conversation. I think a couple of the lads would have stashed a couple of cans of beer in their bags and will have planned on having a sly drink but George wouldn't have been having any of that.

Having a couple of drinks wasn't allowed strictly speaking but I think Denis was savvy enough to know it was going on and as it wasn't anything over the top he let it slide. If anything it helped some of the lads get in the right frame of mind but even if I had fancied a drink George would have put a block on it because he wanted me to make him a cup of tea and run him a bath. He was an immaculate bloke and was very meticulous in his routine, he watched Coronation Street, had his bath and then did his hair with this little comb before turning to me and saying "right, lights out Dickie". This was only at about half past eight, yet he went down with his arms folded across his chest like a mummy and went straight to sleep, he was out and I was left not wanting to cause a fuss so just having to sit in silence.

At seven o'clock sharp his alarm went off and he was straight up out of bed and there was not one hair out of place on his head. I'd been twisting and turning all night but he hadn't even flinched, and it was the same routine as the previous night; "Dickie, run me a bath and make me a cup of tea". The squad then went for a walk and had breakfast together before going to our rooms to kill a bit of time and I was bored stiff, I just kept thinking that it would be a nightmare if I had to put up with it every away game, but that was probably why Denis put me in with him in the first place.

I don't think at the time that teams really looked at the opposition and certainly I don't remember anybody seeing me as a newcomer and targeting me in games. There are scouts at every game now and even at that level the goals are shown on television so everybody knows who you are these days, but I came in under the radar to do well and Denis said as much, but I was out of the team when Benno came back. Just before my debut I had signed an improved contact that would keep me at Sunderland until at least 1990 though so I was able to take it on the chin and knew I would get more chances.

I hadn't really expected to have been thrust into that situation anyway so I took my time on the pitch as a bonus. I was still being selected in the squads and getting named as a sub in some matches, and I was training with the first team so I just took it for what it was, a great experience. I was just glad to be involved then because a year and a half before I was still at school and now I had played for the club I adored. Things seemed surreal, especially the debut itself, it didn't feel as if it was me somehow because it had seemed like only yesterday that I was getting on the bus to come and watch the games as a fan. I kept thinking to myself that it wasn't really happening and I genuinely would wake up on occasions and think to myself 'have I been dreaming?'

I came back into the side after the New Year. The lads had a game down at Bristol Rovers and then travelled straight to Aldershot three days later, and whilst I wasn't in the original group Smithy called Paul Lemon and me up in between because we got turned over in the first one and he wanted to shake things up a little bit. Jack played a lot that season and the next and he was always ribbed off the rest of the squad because he was dating a lass whose Dad worked behind the scenes at Roker Park, but we had to take three different trains just to meet up with the squad and it felt like we were going to the furthest place on earth from Sunderland; God only knows how I would have coped had that rumoured move to Portsmouth gone through.

Denis didn't put me in the starting team and we lost 3-2, but I did come on for my first appearance as a substitute when I replaced Atky. That was February and in April I got another couple of games from the bench before being selected for the trip to Wembley to play in the Mercantile Credit Football Festival, which was part of the Football League's centenary events. At the time I am not sure everybody even knew how we had qualified for an invite and it is not something that many people remember now, but the club took it seriously and we made a big thing of it by travelling down early to get plenty of training in before hand.

We were all given club suits and most of the staff and directors went down to London with us. Chris McMenemy was still involved with the coaching side of things and I remember him talking to me before hand to try and settle me down. The ground wasn't full, but there was still a fair crowd in and we played twenty minutes each half against Wigan Athletic. We played them twice in the league that season and beat them at home and drew at their place but they beat us on sudden death penalties in this one after the game finished 0-0 and that was it, we were out.

There were a lot of Sunderland fans that went all the way down to watch us and they ended up seeing us in action for less than an hour, but people were encouraged to stay all day to watch the other matches and it was seen as an occasion, so the atmosphere was very good. Walking out at Wembley is one of those things you wish for as a boy playing in the street and although the match was a bit unusual due to format I had a good game. I was a bundle of nerves but I got my first touch early on and without really thinking I took the ball down and turned somebody so it settled me down - it was always important to get involved early on and to be sure footed and it set me up for the rest of the match.

Although the game was shortened we played across the full pitch. You were always told that the grass at Wembley would take it out of you, and to be fair it did. I came off afterwards feeling really tired, perhaps more so that after a regular game, and I think the rest of the side were all the same. It's perhaps just as well that I wasn't due to take a penalty, but poor old Colin Pascoe did and it was saved, so when Wigan scored the next one we were knocked out. We really had taken it seriously so to fall at the first hurdle was a blow, and as you would expect we were gutted. Colin had only just got to the club and was a good little player, but we hadn't performed as well as we'd have hoped so the day was a real let down.

I roomed with John Cornforth for the tournament, and during the build up we were lying down on our beds when he got me with one of the oldest tricks in the book.

A maid had been and left some boiled sweets on our bedside cabinets, and because I couldn't find the remote Corny picked one up and asked what channel I wanted on. It was on old fashioned thing with these little black buttons down one side and me being naive and stupid just said "put channel three on" and of course he throws the sweet towards it and sure enough it suddenly came on.

I was amazed and went into fits of laughter. After I settled down he reckoned he was bored of whatever we were watching and asked if he can turn it over so it was the same thing again, he throws a sweet at the set and the channel changes. I was rolling off the bed thinking it was brilliant and because the other lads heard me they came in wanting to find out what is going on. Bearing in mind I was at the other side of the room all he had to do was throw towards the vicinity of the television, but of course everybody else knew the score so when he pretended to do it again they clocked that the remote was hidden down by his side and I was the butt of the gags for the rest of the day.

I don't think Corny meant any harm by it though, I was a first teamer but still quite wet behind the ears and it was good in a way to be part of the group; and whilst it was now clear to me that he was a bit of a joker I knew that he was a really talented lad. He could see a pass and did quite well in the games he got but I think Denis had it in his mind that he didn't have the pace for the top level and didn't fancy him, so he was sold a couple of years later and spent a lot of time playing for Swansea. Sunderland was all still new to Denis really and he was working his way through the squad, he and Viv were quite a youthful management team and had cut their teeth at York but I think Bob Murray had employed them partially on potential having seen something in them and it worked quickly for Sunderland.

Denis was very confident in his own ability and could be quite arrogant at times, whilst Buzzer was more jovial. You could go to him with something and if he didn't think Denis needed to know he would keep it to himself and as a pair the balance was great. Buzzer would have me back for extra training sessions if he thought I needed it, but it would always be done in a positive way and I think their approach had a big impact on the squad and was the main factor in taking us straight back up as champions that season.

Losing at Wembley was tough of course, but it didn't affect our league form and I was an unused sub the night we won the Division Three title against Northampton Town. It was another night game and I was out on the pitch when we were presented with the trophy afterwards, so as we did a lap of honour I was as proud as anything. In the changing room afterwards everybody was partying yet Gordon Armstrong made a point of coming over and saying how well I had been doing, he said he thought I was good enough to play for England one day and to hear that from somebody more senior than me was brilliant.

The season ended at Rotherham United and that was a great day. For me personally it had been a season of new experiences but the club as a whole had been successful too, we had thousands of fans down with us and the party was in full swing. People were hanging off pillars and climbing the stands to get a good view - they were wonderful scenes but were a million miles away from how people attend games now. I was brought on as a substitute and enjoyed another first, although I am never sure whether I should be pleased about being the first Sunderland substitute to ever get replaced himself!

To be fair to myself there was not much I could do as I got a boot in the face I think and was knocked out cold. My excuse of course is that it was the first season that clubs were allowed to name two substitutes but still it's not a very good fact even though there was nothing I could do. I'd come on for Jack and then got replaced by Keith Bertschin who got a couple of goals but I'd come round by the end of the game and as you didn't get taken to hospital in those days I was able to take part in the celebrations. It was mental really; people were hanging over the fences just to shake our hands.

Concussion or not, that season couldn't have gone much better; I was finding my feet and Sunderland were back from the dead. Gary was an established member of the team and we had started rooming together on away trips, we were already close but it was starting to get a bit like the 'Ord and Owers Show' and we could be as thick as thieves when we wanted. The only time we were apart really was when the squad had a night out on the town, Owersy was always more outgoing than me but even during the promotion run in when everybody was enjoying themselves I was still going straight home after games. Things started to change the following season.

Denis handed me my debut, but things then went badly wrong

CHAPTER SEVEN

What goes up must come down

Sunderland were back in Division Two and Smithy and Buzzer could do no wrong. The majority of McMenemy's poorer signings had been moved on and what little money there was had been well spent. It goes without saying that the mood was totally different and whilst I don't feel they instilled a drinking culture as such, they both liked a beer and encouraged everybody to enjoy themselves once training was done.

This was the time when I first started having a few drinks myself; it was perhaps inevitable given the environment I was in and the arrival of Billy Whitehurst early in the season certainly was a factor also. Billy was another senior pro that you could say tried to take me under their wing a bit and he was the best trainer I have ever seen in my life, which was amazing because he seemed to be out getting plastered every night drinking 'BMW's', which is Baileys, Malibu and whisky, and yet he would still be the front runner the next morning.

Ian Botham was a close pal of his so when Beefy had an injury and was looking to do some rehab Billy invited him up to Sunderland. Beefy is a cricketing legend and is a bit of a hero to me and Pratty so we where over the moon about it because we adored him, but the pair of them were always going out on the town and there would be hell on by the end of the night so the Club soon had to put a stop to it all. You heard all sorts of stories about Billy and knowing him they may have been true, but the one that sticks out was about him and Beefy tackling a group of bouncers outside Chambers nightclub and whilst we all had a laugh about it I don't think it was doing the club's reputation any good so it was no wonder the club had to step in.

Denis was a big fan of cricket as well and wasn't a bad turn himself. It always makes me laugh to think about the time he brought all of the first team through to my old stomping ground at Murton Cricket Club to give them a game because he took it so seriously it was unreal. We put them into bat and Denis insisted on having the first bowl, so he walked all the way down the pitch and started making a marker by the side screens. We were all thinking that he couldn't have been planning on running in from all the way back there but sure enough he came pounding in, left arm over and to be fair he was decent; he had good pace and everything, but this was meant to be a Family Fun Day and he was playing as it if was a Test! Owersy and I spent the day laughing at him but there was no let up at all.

Keith Bertschin was another one, he liked a bit of cricket too. He actually left a few weeks before Billy came in but whilst he was here we took on Sunderland Cricket Club at Ashbrooke. The game was for charity and the place was packed; it's quite a big place and I bet there were a few thousand people there. Sunderland had a good side so the standard was high but I got 80 odd and we actually beat them; Iain Hesford got very close to playing first class cricket I believe and he was behind the stumps, and one or two of the other lads had played a bit when they were growing up so it was not like we were no hopers.

Nobody knew that much about Keith as he was a quiet fella but he fancied himself as a cricketer and he wanted to bowl a few over's left arm over, just like Denis. His first ball hit this lad flush on the pads, so Keith turns to the umpire and asks "Owzat??" in this mild Cockney accent, but all he got back was "not out". So he comes in again and the same thing happens; he got this lad on his pads but this time turns round and shouts that loudly that this old umpire jumped back and nearly fell over!

He still wouldn't give it out though and the crowd were falling about laughing because Keith was going berserk. Sure enough the next ball came in and Keith still had the batsman all tied up and we couldn't believe it, the umpire still stood there shaking his head. This time Keith really lost it and was 'effing and blinding; the umpire was a good age and the guy nearly had a heart attack I reckon. The rest of us enjoyed the day though and the club approached me afterwards and asked if I fancied turning out for them, but Smithy put a block on it so it was my last proper game of cricket for a long while, and I doubt the umpire carried on much longer after that either!

Billy and Iain left at the same time as part of the deal that brought Tony Norman to the club, which is perhaps ironic because Tony eventually became a policeman when he left the game and Billy was probably keen to avoid them! Tony was a quality goalkeeper but after promotion we had a hitty missy season back in Division Two. I actually started the first three Northern Intermediate League games of the season because the Central League didn't start until the end of August but from October onwards I was a regular in the first team and I felt quite established. I was only ever out of the side through injury and it was always soft tissue difficulties connected with my growth that were causing the problems; which I found was to become a recurring theme throughout my career.

When I got back to fitness though I would be back in the team; Denis would play three at the back quite a lot then and I usually played in the middle between Monty and Benno, who also had a few injuries and didn't return until the New Year. It was probably the best position I could be asked to play because I could see everything and get the ball out and pass it; I was asked to play like a sweeper really and it was a formation that Denis liked using that season. Having three centre backs was a new thing that was coming into the game so a few sides were trying it and I fitted the bill perfectly for that style of play; I was first asked to play in a couple of those reserve team games at the start of the season and it was like water off a ducks back.

We were still a relatively young side so we had a lot of learning to do but compared to our last two seasons at this level people mostly accepted it as progress. Tony was on form and Marco was getting even more attention and back on a personal level, things seemed to be getting better all of the time too; I'd got my first house up at the top end of Murton and that season saw my first goal for the club.

The house was a little bungalow and for the first six or so months everybody else moved in with me so things were just the same as ever. Mam and Dad had bought my Gran's house when she needed to go into a Home and they were busy doing it up so came in with me in the meantime, but whilst things were a little tight it was never a hindrance. I would have been in no position to complain anyway given the way they had brought me up and how much of an influence they had been on my career; not only was I a regular I was now a goal scorer too!

We were at home to Portsmouth on New Years Eve and if I remember rightly Kevin Ball was actually playing against us that day. We had a free kick and it was taken quickly off the cuff, so I'd only just got into the box from the centre half position as Owersy crossed the ball in first time and Gatesy flicked it towards the goal. I'd continued my run and glanced it into the corner and that was it, I went off running around going mental. Gatesy had already scored earlier in the game and was running back for the restart shouting '"get in" though as if he had scored and I was thinking 'what's he on about?'

The goal was that close to half time that the ref blew the whistle for half time, which was just as well because I needed a rest after all the running around I did celebrating, and as we were going down the tunnel it was announced over the Tannoy system that 'the scorer of Sunderland's second goal is Richard Ord' and Gatesy just went nuts. I've still got the goal on video and the guy doing commentary for the club was an old teacher of mine called Mr Pearson, and he was as pleased as me by the sounds of it, but even on the footage you can see Gatesy shouting at me. He had fallen over after knocking it on so I don't think he saw my touch and he really was going mental telling me it was his, and of course all the others lads were egging him on saying I was nowhere near it even though they knew it was mine.

It was that quick I just did it through instinct, I was right in line with the post so it would have gone wide I think had I not got to it and because it was my first goal I stood my ground. You'd think he would have been over the moon for a young lad to have got his first goal but strikers have that selfishness in them and he was calling me all the names during the half time break; he could be a fiery character but his heart was in the right place and when the penny dropped he came over and finally said "great goal son".

We went on to win the game comfortably 4-0 and after all the carry on with my first goal I went and made sure the next week and got another one in the FA Cup to put us 1-0 against Oxford United. Mam has a great photo of it; Gordon Armstrong took a corner and I was at the near stick in front of the Roker End to guide it in, but I didn't get the chance to go mental because Benno came from nowhere and jumped on me! Oxford equalised in the second half however and we ended up losing to them in the replay on the Wednesday before having them back up here the following Saturday in the league. We won that match but I only got on the score sheet once more in the next four years; I was tall and obviously centre halfs would go up for corners so if you ask me I should have got more goals in my career, but at least I can say I have scored for Sunderland and I am proud of that.

I am also proud to say that I was voted Young Player of the Season for that first campaign back in Division Two. There was always a big do in the suites at Roker Park, and Gabbers got the senior award that same night. Typical me, I was as nervous as anything before the event because of the speech but it was a great night after that was out of the way and bearing in mind it was only my second season I was thrilled. I doubt many people have then gone on to win the senior award, and I have to be honest and say there was a long period after that where I never felt like I was going to achieve the double because whilst 1988-89 had been another good season for me the honeymoon period was soon to be over and I was about to hit my first rocky patch; and it seemed to last for years.

The start of the new decade saw Sunderland eventually, and I mean eventually, go back up to the first division so it was another great time for the club. For me personally though things started to go wrong for the first time as injuries and loss of confidence started to bite. It later proved to be the case that I had played more games in the previous season than the following three put together and it was a first for me to struggle. I had gone from school to the first team pretty swiftly and whilst nothing had been easy as such I had avoided any major disappointments or set backs and found this new situation hard to deal with.

We had started with a great win down at Swindon Town and would prove to be very good on the road all season, but we got turned over against Ipswich Town in our first home game and after being brought into the team I had dropped a massive clanger that had led to one of their goals. I was feeling full of confidence at that point but I dallied a bit on the ball in the last third of the pitch and a lad called David Lowe nicked it off me and scored. Everybody had expected us to win and suddenly we'd conceded four at home, so there was a bit of an uproar and Smith dropped me just like that.

There was no explanation or conversation about it, nothing. Obviously I knew I had mucked up but I was still a young kid and could have done with him sticking by me; I didn't know what to think or how to react and instead of getting the mistake out of my system quickly I ended up dwelling on it. Denis had put his faith in me leading up to that and then after only one real error in approaching 50 senior games I was cast aside and not knowing where I stood because he had me training with the reserves nearly all of the time. It was a failing of his I suppose; I hadn't seen it before because everything had been rosy but his man management wasn't the best in my opinion and I was gutted. Had he taken me out of the firing line for just a couple of games only I could have perhaps understood, but things just got worse and I found it hard to lift myself off the floor; I seemed to play well in the reserves, get an injury, come back and get another injury again.

This lasted for a few months as by then Smith was back to playing two in central defence and Monty and Benno were doing well as a partnership. I got another run in the first team through November when Monty picked up an injury but again, despite feeling as if I had been doing well I was soon out of the team without much explanation and even Reuben Agboola, who was seen more as a full back, got a couple of games ahead of me before Monty returned to the side. We seemed to have a lot of fixtures in that period so I played a lot of games in quick succession and I felt as if I had done enough to justify my place; it had been fair enough that Smithy wanted to take me out of the side after I'd first made my debut when other players were available again but I was an established player now and it didn't make sense.

I did at least get another goal during that spell and it was again at Roker Park, when we won 3-1 against Plymouth Argyle. I'd timed my run perfectly to meet a cross from Gabbers from the left and I powered it into the Fulwell End goal. It was another one of them where I just went berserk; I was running up the touchline and all sorts and it turned out to be a good day because Owersy scored too and afterwards we all went upstairs into one of the Main Stand suites because Benno was having his engagement party.

My celebrations after the goal were probably a mixture of happiness and relief. I had been wound up by the way I was being treated and getting back into the side and playing my part was all I wanted to do. Being out of the side again soon afterwards though, when I didn't really have an idea why, left me feeling up in the air and with their being no guarantee of me getting another game anytime soon I ended up going to York City in February 1990; but what had initially seemed like being a good idea proved to be just another cause of frustration.

I went out on loan shortly after Tommy Lynch did, but whilst he ended up making his switch to Shrewsbury permanent and had a very good spell there my move didn't help me kick on the way I hoped. A lot of Denis' buys proved to be successful at

Sunderland but it never worked out in poor Tommy's case and I think part of it was down to him having a shaky first couple of games. He arrived from Ireland just before the previous season started and because Denis had him doing everything in training, free kicks, corners, the lot, we were all joking on that Tommy must have been from a tough family or something and that they had threatened him or something. Come his debut though and bless him, he had a nightmare I felt; even his throw ins were bad so he was soon out of the side and we were all kidding Smithy on that some Irish blokes had been in looking for him and all of this, trying to wind him up.

John Bird was the manager of York and I found out that initially he had actually rang Denis to see if he could have Micky Heathcote back on loan but because he'd had a slight injury Denis suggested to John that he took me instead. I'd formed a good reputation the season prior and even as early as that had been linked with an England Under 21 call up within some circles so John apparently asked if Denis was sure because he couldn't quite believe I was being made available. That alone shows how my stock had fallen within the club but I tell you what, no matter how difficult I thought things were at Sunderland going down to Bootham Crescent to play in Division Four was still a massive culture shock.

With York being as close as it is I was still at my own home and just driving down every morning. Training was held on a school field and the lads had to bring their own kit with them; I don't want to sound as if I was above my station or anything like that but these were just not things I was used to. It was not what I expected and from that point I wished I had never agreed to it; although I think now that had I known what the situation was going to be like I might have been prepared and handled it better.

The blokes already there were mainly journeymen pros really and Bird was old school in his approach. He had been a defender himself and was at Newcastle United as a player but was still quite new to management after being in charge at Hartlepool United for a couple of seasons before coming to York City. My debut was at home against Scarborough, which was a bit of a derby, and it was the first time I had ever seen a bottle of whisky put in front of the players in the changing rooms before kick off. Although I had started drinking on nights out there was no way I was going to have any before a game and yet it was being hoyed in my face. All of the other lads were taking swigs to settle their nerves but I just said "no chance". It opened my eyes and I doubt my reaction made me the most popular.

I was playing alongside a guy called Ray Warburton, who was in his first full season as a professional. It was a horrible day weather wise, the pitch was horrendous and we lost 2-1 but during that first game the thing I remember most was taking the ball down and passing it along the floor like I was used to doing day in day out in training but just getting a massive ticking off from Bird for it. He didn't want me to do anything else like that and just yelled at me "kick it as far as you can" whenever I got the ball after that; it was all about us humping it long and anything else was seen as messing about.

The same thing happened again two weeks later at Exeter City, I just did things naturally but Bird didn't want me taking what he saw as being risks. My partner in central defence this time was Ricky Greenough yet we lost again, but it was actually an entertaining game because they were one of the few sides that try to get the ball down and pass it around. Their style suited me and I gave a good performance but it didn't save me from getting told off afterwards.

We were scheduled to travel there and back all in the same day, which I couldn't believe. We arrived back and from York I got straight in my car and drove back home to Murton. The match had been on the same day as my 20th birthday and I got back home during the silly hours in the morning so was sat up on my own opening my presents, feeling miserable. I just felt it wasn't ever going to work so on the following Monday morning I saw Denis and said I was having doubts.

I had a bit of a change of heart though and decided to give it another go in the game at Wrexham that midweek. It was another long journey though, another partner in defence and another defeat. Ricky wasn't at York all that long and might have gone into non league football after that, and whilst Steve Tutill, who I was alongside against Wrexham, was a York lad that went on to play for the club for years he was still quite inexperienced at that time also. I had been frozen out at Sunderland and had felt that going on loan might boost my prospects a bit but I wasn't doing what they wanted and they weren't helping me in any way either so I saw Denis again and told him I had made my mind up.

Denis didn't really say much about it after that, York came on the phone trying to chase me a couple of times but Sunderland were paying my wages anyway I think and it just wasn't proving worthwhile. Denis and Viv had done a great job there and were seen as legends around the place so were happy to do York a favour but it wasn't for me, I wasn't learning anything by trying to lump the ball and I felt uncomfortable throughout my time there.

Even then it was preached by Sunderland to pass the ball to feet when it was appropriate. That has always been my philosophy and it was why Reidy was such a big influence on my career because that was what he liked me to do. His younger brother Shaun was at York the same time as me and so was Ricky Sbragia, who worked mainly with the youth side but then came to Sunderland for the first time later that decade and was part of the coaching staff alongside Sacko, who oddly enough was the man John Bird replaced at Bootham Crescent.

After York it was just back to the reserves for me. I expected it to be honest, the lads were flying and I had not pulled up any trees down there so at least I was able to accept not being in the team anymore. It was before then that killed me, even Denis would admit that central defenders do not come of age until later in their career and he knew mistakes would be made, but it is how players are allowed to react and learn that makes the difference. I had not been making a habit of daft errors or costing us points and yet after being a regular the season before I was now the forgotten man.

Denis liked me to keep possession; he encouraged me to pass to a man, so it was not like at York where my style didn't suit the tactics or the team so after first being dropped I was never sure what was wanted from me. That was the downside to playing under Denis I thought, nobody enjoys being out of the team anyway but the communication was missing and I have since told him that to his face. I didn't have the balls to do it at the time but I honestly felt then, and still do, that he should have stuck by me because for a good few seasons my confidence was shot and I was poorer as a player; it was that serious.

At least I was still being involved in the squads and travelling with the first team to some of the away games. Our away form was a large part of us reaching the Play Offs that season and those two infamous matches against Newcastle United. I was actually in with the Sunderland fans along side a couple of mates for the second leg at St James' Park when we won 2-0 and there were one or two people turning round and asking what I was doing there. I was still a fan no matter what issues I was having though and wanted us to win as much as the next man.

In the lead up to the Play Off Final Denis took us all to Minorca but for me it was a ridiculous idea, Denis basically said 'on you go lads' and it was not the best way to prepare by any stretch of the imagination. Denis and Buzzer liked to have a beer or two with us on occasion but some of the lads were on the drink for days solid, so who do you blame? Under some regimes or before certain games no alcohol is allowed and then at other times people can get away with almost anything.

It's hard to believe now that I spent over a year on that frame...

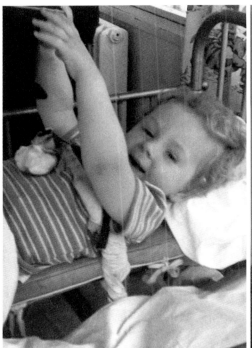

That's me, aged six

Practising for all those squad photographs; back row, fourth from the left

My first year at school

A presentation at Murton County Primary School

And here I am with the rest of the side, holding the trophy

Dodi and Gran had their troubles, but Gran was always there for us when I was growing up

Dad (left) has always been a massive Sunderland fan too, and he loves talking about the greats. Here he's chatting to one of his favourites, Jimmy McNab

Mam and Dad have always been by my side

I felt just as comfortable playing cricket
when I was young as I did football,
and I still love the sport now

Fresh faced and about to become a first team regular

Learning my trade; an early game at centre back at the Northumbria Centre

Another picture from my early days as a pro

Thanks for everything Mam and Dad

Cheers! Pratty and I enjoy a beer

Players are adults and should be treated as so, but they need focus too in some situations and if boundaries and routines are not in place some go crazy. Yes, you need an element of self control but if you are nervous say before a big game and there is nothing to occupy your time it is easy to guess how people will react.

Admittedly, after a long season there was little point in working the lads too hard in training and I suppose the thinking behind going away was to allow everybody to switch off and get rid of some stress but the balance wasn't right. I was sharing with Gary, but he was having a few issues back home so was in a sulk and barely left our hotel room, and I could have done with him backing me up and telling me to keep my mouth shut because I ended up getting into a bit of bother on one of the nights out.

We were in some bar cracking on and I must have been having a whinge about Denis. You do get that sometimes and it was not something that was seen as out of place but the next morning I was woken up by Smithy banging on the door. He just said to me "I want a word with you, now" and I have to admit that my face dropped, but he just wanted to go for a walk down on the beach and he actually explained for the first time what his thoughts were about my situation, he even said "I still love you as a player and I want you to keep going" and at least it took away a bit of the uncertainty.

It should have happened a long time before that though and what I didn't like was the way that it came about; it turned out that somebody had gone running off to Denis telling him I was rocking the boat and slagging him off and rather than clearing the air it made me look bad. I didn't really mean anything by it; everybody has a moan when they are not in the team and it is one of those unwritten laws that what gets said in the changing room or between the lads should be kept private.

I was a bit annoyed with myself too because I'd been keeping my head down before that and was working as hard as I could in training. I was not somebody that would have knocked on the managers door looking for a showdown, maybe I should have done in that situation given the knock on effect it had, but I think the fact I had missed out on the promotion push was hard to take so was just letting off steam.

Despite the pep talk on the beach I wasn't even in the squad come the Play Off Final against Swindon Town and I had to travel to London on a separate bus to the first team. My fiancée Nicola and the other wives and girlfriends came down with us and we were even staying in a different hotel. We had a good time to be honest because we didn't have to prepare for the game, although I was not in the best of moods at all so probably brought the rest of the group down a bit.

Ricardo Gabbiadini was one of the other lads that I spent a bit of time with on that trip and he was always a good laugh when we went away, not least because he was as clumsy as anything. We'd twice been to Yugoslavia to take part in a youth tournament and roomed together on the trip, but after leaving the hotel one evening to go on a night out we ended up going back with a couple of girls to their room because Ricardo had been trying to chat one of them up. He went into the en suite though and suddenly we heard this massive crash; I jumped up to see what had happened and somehow he'd managed to pull the sink from the wall and there was water gushing everywhere. The next thing we know there is hotel staff banging on the door trying to find out what was going on so we had to duck out through the window and ended up doing a runner through the streets of Pula all because of him.

Even though he was a lovely bloke the rest of the lads knew exactly what he was like too and he was always getting himself into these daft situations. We were doing a couple of drills at the training ground once and true to form, he overran the ball and it ended up in a load of wild bushes at the top of the pitches. He had to go and try to get the ball back and sure enough he ended up getting stuck in there; all you could see was this bush moving and shaking and everybody was too busy laughing to go and help him so he ended up being nicknamed the Singing Bush from then on.

As for the game itself, we were battered and Gary in particular was absolutely distraught afterwards because he thought his big chance of Division One had gone. Swindon were a hell of a passing side at the time and we did well to hang in and keep it at 1-0, but then of course we got that unusual reprieve when Swindon were found guilty of 'financial irregularities' and we were to go up instead. There had been rumours about it within the club before the game actually, but obviously the match had to go ahead as normal and at that point I don't think I had seen Owersy as upset, and I dare say the Swindon players must have found it a very difficult situation to deal with too when the decision was made.

All that was to happen down the line in the summer however; immediately after there had been a dinner arranged with our partners and Nicola and I happened to be sat with Denis. We spoke at length again and he told me that he wanted me to have a really good go the following season. I don't know what prompted it, maybe he felt bad about not talking to me sooner perhaps, but I have to admit that it was good to hear; it had been an awful season for me and this was the light at the end of the tunnel I needed going into the summer.

Division One here we come

CHAPTER EIGHT

The Black Cat and the Three Lions

The start of pre season training for the 1990-91 campaign saw everybody on a high. Promotion had been confirmed in the end and as I was desperate to turn my own situation round and be part of the action again I made sure that I turned up the fittest I had even been. Just as had been the case the year before however, my high hopes were soon to be dashed.

Nicola and I had a week away on holiday but other than that I really put the work in. I was going for runs, keeping off the drink, everything, and I think it surprised the lads to see me leading the way when it came to our early training sessions. I was flying, and felt good in our warm up games too; we played Torpedo Moscow at Roker Park a couple of weeks before the start of the season and I put in a great performance. The Russians were very good technically, but I had been used as a sweeper and snuffed a lot of their attacks out, and at that point Denis even went as far as coming out and saying in the papers that it was going to be hard to leave me out of the side once the league fixtures started.

You learn not to take anything for granted in football, but people were coming up to me and saying they had never seen me play so well in my life and I really did think to myself 'I'm in here'. Come the first game of the season at Norwich City though and I wasn't even in the squad; the list got put up on the wall and I couldn't believe it. I was doing what Denis had asked, I was on top of my game, and it still wasn't good enough. It felt like a massive kick in the teeth; my confidence had been creeping back yet this floored me and I was back to square one.

What made it harder to take was that Monty had endured a bit of a shocker during pre season but was still in ahead of me for that one game, only for Smithy to then move him on afterwards. I ended up playing for the reserves at Hartlepool United instead and wouldn't you know it, I ended up getting injured.

After half an hour or so I went over on my ankle and sprained it. Just days before things had been looking up, but now I was left thinking 'what's just happened to me?' Next up were Tottenham Hotspur and because this was in the aftermath of Italia '90 and they had Gary Lineker and Paul Gascoigne in the side it was a big deal. Gazza was thought of as the biggest thing since sliced bread but he got a bit of stick from the Sunderland fans because of his Newcastle connections, and of course the atmosphere was electric given it was our first home game back in the big league.

Like Monty, Kevin Ball had struggled initially during his first pre season at the club but because I'd done my ankle he got the nod to start; he was outstanding in that match and never looked back from there. Bally always likes to joke on to people that he only got to know me later down the line when we were lagging behind everybody else during training runs, but with Denis not given the funds he would have liked he could only afford then to bring him and Peter Davenport into the squad.

We were fairly confident though, Dav was a well know player and people like Gary and Marco were hot property. By the time I was back to fitness we were five games into the season and I got my first appearance away at Wimbledon. I was used as a sweeper again when I had played midweek for the reserves, and because I got through it okay Denis' plan was to put me there against Wimbledon as it would help combat the long ball tactic and protect the back four as at that time they were packed with big, strong lads like John Fashanu and John Gayle, who had previously been working as a builder before becoming a professional, and he knew it was going to be a scrap.

Wimbledon were still playing home games at Plough Lane and when we arrived you could hear the music pumping out of the changing rooms. Everything was in your face, trying to unsettle you, and all they did was lump the ball long all game. Teams couldn't handle it when they banged the ball forward so they were full of energy and within ten minutes I was lying flat out on the deck after being elbowed by Gayle. As I sat up he raked his boot down my spine for good measure, but when I turned round to call him something he just walked away laughing.

In the main we stood up to the tactics though and I started playing myself in the game, so of course Fash thought he would have a go instead. He elbowed me in the head and straight away I could feel the blood pouring out; but when he came over instead of asking if I was okay he just put his finger on the cut, licked it and said something like 'I love the taste of your blood'. I didn't have a clue what to do at that point but still feel I handled myself well and stood up to the intimidation but after the match I was approached by a couple of the national press writers for interviews, so come the Monday morning The Sun were running the Fash story as their headline; can you imagine that now?

He was just trying to psyche me out and gain an advantage, but there would be hell on I think if that happened today; there would be all sorts of repercussions. As far as we were concerned though, all that mattered was the fact that we gave away two cheap goals late on after Gordon Armstrong and Dav had put us ahead and that was a habit we couldn't shake all season. I then came on as a substitute in midweek when we lost the first leg of a League Cup tie at home to Bristol City, and seven days after that first start against Wimbledon Roker Park was packed again for the visit of Liverpool.

We would go on to the away leg and beat Bristol City comfortably on aggregate, but before that the arrival of the reigning champions was yet another big occasion and it attracted the largest crowd I played in front of at Roker Park. Liverpool had started the season in unbelievable form and here I was having gone so quickly from a bit part squad member to going up against world class players like John Barnes, Peter Beardsley and Ian Rush. A tactical reshuffle meant I was moved to left back and despite not having played there properly at any point in my career and it being a red hot sunny day I barely put a foot wrong and came away getting rave reviews in the press again. Playing against that standard of player seemed unreal, and yet it wasn't something that fazed me much; my problems were more through being in and out of the team and sure enough I was dropped for next match away at Villa.

It was another case of me having played well but Smith not seeing that way, and instead he gave Anthony Smith his debut whilst I sat on the bench and we ended up losing 3-0. I was an unused substitute throughout November too and only ended up making 14 league appearances in total, but as we had a good reserve team at that time whenever I was needed I could step right back in and even at left back felt comfortable at that level. No matter how good an account of myself I felt I gave however I was dropped as soon as somebody else became available and the situation was no different to how it had been the season before.

We didn't get turned over all that often during that top flight campaign but we were in the relegation zone from March onwards. The last home game of the season was against Arsenal and there was a lot riding on it, because they were going for the title and we could still save ourselves from a quick return to Division Two. The match was shown on ITV but I wasn't playing so it was club suit and tickets in the seating area for me. Gary wasn't looking forward to it either because it was going to be one of the first times he had been interviewed live on the television but did really well in the game and if it wasn't for David Seaman sticking his hand out and making a brilliant save Gary would have scored a great goal after beating a couple of defenders and hitting a curling shot. Everybody thought it was in, but Seaman made the save and Gary had to get through his interview nervously with me laughing in the background.

Arsenal went on to win the title so to get a draw against them showed that we weren't that far off the standard needed, but we still had to beat Manchester City the following week and hope that Derby County could do us a favour against Luton Town if we were going to stay up. Niall Quinn was playing for City that day and because Bally was out I came into the middle of defence up against him. The amount of fans we took down was incredible, it showed people exactly what Sunderland is all about and I think that must have had some sort of impact on Quinny because of course he went on to have such a connection with the Sunderland supporters.

The game itself was a very tense affair, and as always it seemed to be the case with Sunderland during my time that we had something to play for at the end of the season so the lads were very nervous before hand. There were lots of games that season where we played well or went ahead, but we were quite a young side and were very naive at times. That was the case against City too, we were ahead at one stage and still lost and that inability to see things out was what did us because I don't think we were out of our depth quality wise; we weren't a bad side and managed to go to places and give teams a game but it wasn't enough to just play pretty football and after all the rebuilding under Smith, Sunderland were going back down again.

The fans refused to leave the ground until we came back out and they had been given the opportunity to applaud us, and they did it to a man because I think they could see how much we had tried and that relegation wasn't through a lack of effort. Gary never missed a game that season and was devastated, and it took us all a while to get over it emotionally because we had been almost there as a side. Straight after the game we were scheduled to go to Ibiza though because the trip had already been arranged, and whilst none of us felt in the mood for it at first it was probably the best thing we could have done as we ended up having a massive blow out and managed to block everything out for a few days.

Before setting off Benno said he was going for a haircut but he never turned up for the bus and we had to leave him behind otherwise we'd have missed the flight. He was from Manchester of course so probably ended up at one of his old haunts, but we never found out what went on; we just knew that with him being club captain it didn't go down too well in some quarters and there was hell on about it after the summer. I think Owersy and I were getting a bit of a reputation as the 'terrible twosome' when we were out on the drink then too and with it being a big part of the culture around football I got sucked in and made the most of Ibiza; the place was wild.

It's seen as being old school now, but I can honestly say that at least we would only have a session at weekends or after games. It was probably to be expected when you had young lads with a bit of money trying to forget their troubles back home and over there some of the dafter lads were in their element.

Attitudes have changed a lot since then, perhaps because of situations where talented players did not always go on to make the most of their ability, but if you'd seen me over in Ibiza at the time you would have struggled to believe I was gearing up for a tour with the England Under 21s squad either having made my Three Lions debut earlier in the season.

My name had been linked with a call up in previous seasons but my involvement started a couple of months into the relegation season when Denis pulled me and Brian Atkinson just before training one morning and told us that we had both been selected, and obviously I was delighted. I had been an outcast for so long and less than a year ago was on loan at York just to get games, and then suddenly I was in the England Under 21s squad so it came as a massive boost too. Of course I was keen to tell my parents as soon as possible and Mam was pleased for both me and Atky because she was quite close with Brian's mother, and in fact a lot of the parents were friendly with each other.

The mothers all went to games together and it must have been stressful at some points watching their own sons, so it was good for them to know other people going through the same thing. They were at one match when some massive bloke in front of them was having a pop at Gordon Armstrong, so his mum stood up and told the guy to watch his mouth. It could have turned nasty but I think he was so shocked and so embarrassed that he just went into his shell, and I think my Mam was tempted to do the same herself on a few occasions during my career but thought better of it.

When you play football people can think you are public property and forget that you have loved ones around you that might not have the thick skin that you do. The club is part of a wider family though and the bond was close at Sunderland, Benno's mum was lovely too and was part of the group even though Benno hadn't come through the ranks like some us had; but she still hit it off with Mam and was just like her son, always immaculate. When she introduced herself as his Mam you had to laugh though - it was clear from a mile off!

One of the reasons I was so proud to have been picked for the Under 21s was because I knew how much it would mean to my family, who had been with me every step of the way. My debut was in December 1990 at Prenton Park and they came down with Nicola to watch me, and so did Denis and Viv. Ray Harford was in charge but Graham Taylor and Lawrie McMenemy were there in the changing room before hand too because they were running the senior side. They had a quiet word with each of us and again they said the same sort of things at half time, it was only little comments like 'play your usual game', nothing that inspiring or ground breaking really, but at least Lawrie recognised me after getting me to clean his car every week.

Singing the national anthem before hand and what have you was very emotional and although it finished 0-0 it was a good game. We were against Wales and Andy Melville was playing for them, we were both at centre half; it was the first time I had ever seen Mel and he was outstanding, even though he looked about 40 years old because he had a horrible 'tash going on. After that I was selected again for the squad at home to Ireland and away to Turkey but didn't actually play for them again until finishing up in Ibiza and going to the Toulon tournament at the end of the season, which was the same tournament Marco had gone to in 1989 when he was picked for England.

Even though I had drank a bit in Ibiza before joining up with the squad I was young enough to get away with it and was feeling in good shape when we met for the trip. Atky went too and so did my old school teammate Paul Kitson, which was a big thing for somewhere the size of Murton. Alan Shearer was another North East born player in the squad, although he was at Southampton then, and he was already starting to make a name for himself so it meant getting back into the hotel whenever we had been somewhere was always a fight because all the press men would be waiting for him outside.

We had a good squad looking back at some of the names, Shearer became a regular for the senior side and so did Steve McManaman and David James, who you could see was a clever bloke but would then go and do something crazy; we were all on ski lifts once whilst we were out there and because he knew me and Atky didn't like heights he started rocking it like you'd never seen, and yet he could be very thoughtful at other times.

Training was always enjoyable with Ray, and Shearer and I would have quite a bit of banter. I was always telling him that he would never get past me, but he was as dry as sticks and had a sense of humour that people perhaps don't always see. He gave as good as he got, but he was single minded too and didn't care what people thought of him - after the tournament he was going away to get married and of course because we were all young lads we were ribbing him and saying he was being stupid and didn't know what he was doing, but he could be very dismissive; he just ignored people if he needed and has proven to be as strong willed ever since.

There was a kid called Carl Tiler there too and he was one of the lads I was vying with for a place at centre back. He actually left the camp to go and sign for Brian Clough at Nottingham Forest for just under £1.5 million before Clough flew him back again, and it was a big talking point for a youngster to go for that type of cash. I still got to play twice though, once against Mexico and then against the CIS at left back. I had a bit of experience of playing eastern European sides having been to Yugoslavia but I didn't know much about the Mexicans or the way they approached their opponents. I soon found out that they were very technical, but they were small too and here we were, me and Kitson, two lads from Murton lining up for a corner when from nowhere this Mexican starts biting me on the shoulder.

The lad had really sunk his teeth into me and as I was pushing him onto the deck you could see Kitson stood there laughing his head off. Honestly, he was crying with laughter so the guy got up off the floor and spat right in Kitson's face and I started laughing too. With all those reporters there following Shearer and then Tiler the story got in the press back home and one of them did a story with me joking on about how I didn't know how I was going to explain it to Nicola because it looked like a love bite. It was pretty serious though in truth, because we both ended up having to get a tetanus jab afterwards.

We won all three group games 2-1 and I was awarded the Man of the Match award in the two games I played. We topped the group and got into the final against France so in the build up to that had a day off down on the beach with a few drinks. For some daft reason McManaman started insisting that I gave everybody a song so I got up and did my piece and everybody was joining in, even the locals that were down there got involved, and all the while Shearer was just shaking his head calling me a stupid Murton so and so!

Not for the first time in my career though, the favourites got picked for the final and I was gutted because I had done well in my two matches. Chris Vinnicombe was at left back and although he was at a big club in Glasgow Rangers I felt I was miles better than him, and even though everybody had been saying to me that they felt I would play, it was another one of those situations where it counted for nothing. I still hoped to get on though from the bench, it was quite a hostile atmosphere with it being against the French in their own back yard but Shearer scored with just over ten minutes to go and with the clock running down I was told to get my boots on, but the final whistle went before there was a stop in play and I was stood on the touchline ready to go like a tin of spare milk.

It was a shame because it would have been another cap, I got the three I did win framed and they are lovely things. Pratty's kid has one of them on his bedroom wall and they are all treasured, but the same thing happened to me again early the following season and I missed out on another; we beat Germany at Scunthorpe and I was going to come on but didn't manage it before the game finished, maybe they were cost cutting! That was my last chance too as after the Germany friendly I was too old to get selected for the European Championship qualifiers, and back at Sunderland Smithy was about to be shown the exit door too.

Before the England trip going to Ibiza had done us all some good. We returned for pre season though and all the feelings of being back in Division Two resurfaced, and we were sickened. The club had been given a massive opportunity and failed to make the most of it; the game had been in a state and was just starting to pick itself up, and had we stayed up then we could have caught the train and become established in the top flight again.

A lot of clubs wanted Smith and Busby because they were this new partnership that had got results at first but I think Bob just expected them to keep getting players from the youth side and using them. Now for me, that had been great initially and it meant the club had a lot of local lads playing, but every side needs one or two established players as well and that would have made the difference to our time in Division One. The hangover from that was one of the things that held us back in the coming seasons; I had just played in all four divisions in the space of four seasons, but change was something I was soon going to have to get used to even more.

I bet Quinny thought I couldn't see him lurking in the background!

CHAPTER NINE

The managerial merry-go-round starts up

So, not only had my domestic career stalled over the last two seasons but now so too had the club. I think Bob Murray knew that Smithy had done the best he could with the resources he had given him though and with us expected to be one of the front runners in the coming season I don't remember there ever being any question marks over Denis' future at this point.

The players were all confident of coming straight back up after relegation too and Smithy didn't really change the squad over the summer, partly because he was happy with what we had and partly because I don't think he had that much money to play with anyway. Bally had just had a great season and Gabbers was still around but whilst the squad looked good, from my own point of view I was still in the doldrums.

I had played okay in the last game of the season at Manchester City and I remember Smithy having another heart to heart with me when we were in Ibiza where he said that I needed to kick on, but I kept picking up niggling injuries and never seemed to be able to get going. I'd wanted to take that positive experience from Toulon and try and get onto some sort of roll again, but even then my body still seemed to be growing and after starting the first three games of the season I kept picking up random muscular problems like strains or cramps, and every time I came back my body failed me again.

Even though I was relatively young, I had already been through a lot in my career; I had played in a few different positions, had been involved in two promotion campaigns and had played in the top flight, but my experience was no use to anybody if I wasn't available to play games and the timing couldn't have been worse because results hadn't been as good as hoped and we were lurking around the bottom half of the table. The scars of relegation were proving to be deeper than we thought and who knows, Smithy might just have looked to me to freshen things up.

Whether that would have turned out to be the case or not I can't be sure, but it was certainly becoming clear that he was getting a bit desperate. The lads hadn't even been playing all that badly, but the results didn't match and with Gabbers having been sold to fund new arrivals there was even more pressure on Smithy but he just couldn't put a run together to take us away from the clubs at the bottom.

Now we had a little bit of money to spend Denis found it hard to find any value in the transfer market and at first he was unable to bring a new striker in to fill Marco's boots. To fill the gap initially then, he hatched this plan where Benno would be used up front on his own away at Cambridge United and in the days leading up to the game, all Smithy was doing in training was getting the lads to hit it up to Benno.

We'd actually scored four the week before when we played Brighton and Hove Albion but Benno had never been used as a striker in his life and that was the point where most of the lads realised that the game was up for Smithy. With me being injured I didn't even travel down for the game itself but when I spoke to a couple of the boys afterwards it sounded like a disaster. The Cambridge manager John Beck would let the grass grow in the corners of the pitch to try and stop teams that used wingers and he would play for throw ins and free kicks so they could launch the long ball into the box at every opportunity. Smithy went with all of the big lads and tried to do the same thing, but that wasn't fair on Benno and he would have been better off in his usual position because we got thumped.

Funnily enough, Benno did manage to get on the score sheet from defence two games later as we went on a run of scoring seven goals in the next three games but these soon started to dry up after that and whilst he hung around until the Christmas period, most people now felt deep down that Smithy had ran out of ideas despite the fact he eventually managed to sign a couple of new forwards in the shape of John Bryne and Don Goodman. Neither had hit the ground running however; Don was sent off on his debut and whilst John scored two goals on his second appearance for the club as part of that mini goal glut it was only after Denis had left that we saw the best of them.

Rather than that though, it was the departure of Buzzer that proved to be the final straw in my mind. Smithy probably didn't want to be in a position where he had to do it, and even when he came to tell us the news he just looked different somehow. He was wearing a white jumper and I know it sounds like a daft little thing, but it was so out of character for him and before he started speaking you could see all of the other lads looking around at each other and thinking to themselves 'what's going on here'.

The club made some sort of excuse, but I wondered at the time if was just to take the attention off Smith for a bit. I personally thought that they should have gone as a pair, as that was how they came in and that was how I always saw them. It was always Smith that had the final say and made the selections, but they were a team and he needed Buzzer there for his style to work.

Buzzer would always be the one that linked between Smithy and the changing room. He was enthusiastic and obviously knew the game inside out, and he would often tell me to keep going and give me a lift from him when my mood was low. I think most of the other lads liked him too because he had a habit of putting you at ease. The youth tournament in Yugoslavia that I went on with Ricardo was a good example of that, we went there a couple of years in a row and although it was Chris McMenemy that took charge of us Buzzer was with the party as well. They were both interesting trips actually, this was before the troubles over there and it was a beautiful country, but the competition itself attracted a few big name clubs and was of a very high standard so we did well to reach the final one year and win it the other, and I was very honoured to be awarded 'Player of the Tournament' the first time we where there.

The trip was for younger members of the senior squad, so John Cornforth was one of the lads there and his eyes lit up when Chris let us go for a night out, although

Buzzer gave us his usual 'just stick to the halfs please lads' line. That was something you always noticed about Buzzer, he would insist on drinking halfs whereas Smithy stuck to pints; which of course us daft lads did as well on this particular night out without giving it a second thought. We'd ended up in some beach bar and were drinking out of these long tall glasses you could see from a mile off, but just as Buzzer walked round the corner about to catch us all red handed Corny clocked him and shouted out "they sell big halfs in here mind, don't they lads?", and all Viv did was just shrug his shoulders and join in with the drinks.

If anything, the fact that Smithy and Buzzer loved a drink and had brought that freedom into the club did a lot to bring us together as a group, and it worked most of the time. Losing somebody as popular as Buzzer left a gap then, and the move only made matters worse for Smithy I reckon because the dressing room went a bit and it wasn't all that long before he was gone too.

His last game as manager saw us lose away at Oxford United and it was a shame the way things went because we had a decent relationship in my first couple of years as a senior player and I'll always be thankful that he put a bit of faith in me and gave me my debut when he did. I don't even feel as if I had even had a bad game though, I just made the one error and whilst it was admittedly a big one the way I seemed to be given all of the blame set me a long way back and took a long time to fully recover from.

From that point onwards it didn't seem as if he trusted me and I think that showed when he brought out his own autobiography and in talking about his time at Sunderland seemed to point the finger at me for some of our results in Division One. He made reference to the fact that we only won once whilst I was in the team and said how he felt he should have kept Monty on, but I don't think it is fair to pick out one of the younger players when the group as a whole struggled to pick up the wins, and even less so one that played well which ever position I was asked to play in.

Basically, he had helped build me up and then knocked me down and I've always had mixed memories of the guy when I've since looked back. Fans too are maybe the same, as whilst the work he did in getting us back out of Division Three so quickly was very important to the club his star had waned after the start of the 1991-92 season. You see it so many times though, a manager gets the chance to put things right after relegation but if the momentum isn't there and one or two teams raise their game to get one over these supposedly better sides from a higher division it all unravels and the man in charge gets the sack a few months into the new season anyway, and Smith's departure kick started a merry-go-round of internal appointments in the coming seasons.

Malcolm Crosby was the man asked to step in as a caretaker at first, but the fact we won his first four games and went on a run to the FA Cup Final gave Bob Murray little choice to make it a permanent arrangement in the end. I knew Crossa quite well before he got the job, he didn't come in as a youth coach until after I had moved into the seniors but he was still registered as a player for a little while and had a couple of games for the reserves. He was as fit as a lop and was like Buzzer in many ways, he was very enthusiastic and understood the game brilliantly; but once I became available again I barely got a look in.

Crossa too would take me for runs and put on sessions for me when I was looking to come back from injury or do a bit extra on a particular area of my game. With me staying back to work one on one with him with got to know each other quite well and had a good relationship, but when he got the job that soon changed and he seemed to go off me as a player. Why that happened remains a mystery though because he had always told me that I had the ability and appreciated me when he was in charge of the reserves, but he just didn't back it up when he was in a position to use me for the first team.

In fact, quite soon after Smith left Crossa tried to sell me on. I was still out of the picture through injury and so was in the physio room with Steve Smelt when I found out, as he just walked in and came out with it, saying "the Dundee manager has been on the phone, do you want to go?" Apparently they had offered £200,000 for me and Crossa encouraged me to go up to Scotland to talk to them, but it was a no goer for me from the off and I blanked it.

At that point Dundee weren't even in the Scottish Premier League, they did get promotion at the end of the season and were perhaps looking to strengthen in preparation for that but even if they had already been in the top division I wasn't interested in leaving Sunderland so it proved to be a non starter. What it did show to me however, was that despite having thought that I was perhaps going to see a change of luck it was actually the case that I was going to find it just as hard as ever to get back into the manager's plans.

Smith leaving had given me a bit of hope that I could get established in the team again, but I went straight back down again after that little incident. At the time it was between myself and Ian Sampson for places as we played at centre half together for the reserves a bit; it would be one of us that would get called up if there was an injury and I think Crossa preferred him to me. He was a good coach though I must say, some of the sessions I would see him put on for the youth players were excellent - they really were light years ahead of what other clubs were doing and some of the stuff he did then is still all the rage now.

Crossa's problem though, I always felt, was that whilst he was obviously a great coach I never thought he had seen himself becoming a manager. He was a local lad so had the club's best interests at heart, but he just didn't have that edge that you perhaps need and I think that had the cup run not come about and forced everybody's hand he would not have looked to become the gaffer in his own right. As it was, the cup run at least gave the place a badly needed lift and some positive attention even if it did nothing for our league form after the initial improvement.

Being at the club during the road to the final was a difficult period for me if I am being honest. As a fan it was fantastic but as a player, being unable to really do my bit and just having to look on from the sidelines it was frustrating too so me and Owersy, who was also injured a lot in that season, were going out on the town often. The amount of sessions we had was ridiculous really but being on the fringes was so difficult we both felt there was nothing else to do to but try and let it all out.

I did manage one appearance in the cup however and it remains one of the highlights of my career as it was in the quarter final replay against Chelsea at Roker Park. I think a lot of people would agree that the atmosphere was brilliant, and it was definitely the best I ever experienced as a player. A lot of the other lads felt the same too, and it really did make the hairs on the back of your neck stand up. I came on as a substitute and was stood behind Gordon Armstrong as he scored the winner, I think it was Atky that took the corner, and he drilled it across the edge of the box and Gordon got up above his marker to score a perfect header. He was always good in the air, but this was something special even by his standards and nights like that were what Roker Park was all about and to be involved was unforgettable.

I then came back in and played the last league game of the season when we drew 2-2 against Cambridge. It was our fourth draw in a row as a lot of the squad turned their attention to the final but I did well in that game and was gutted to then find that I hadn't even got into the squad for Wembley and that Ian Sampson had been selected ahead of me. Ian was a good honest pro but I thought I was a better player, and as I had done well in the previous game thought I had every chance. When he pinned up the squad list however I was distraught and as had happened before with Denis, Crossa didn't even talk to me about it afterwards or attempt to explain why.

I always knew that being selected to play was going to be a long shot, but to have to travel down on a different bus alongside the other unused players again like I had done two years earlier for the Play Off Final was awful and it didn't feel as if I was attached at all - we went with our partners and had a night out in London like we did before and that was the most enjoyable part of the trip. Crossa must have known how much it would have meant to me, being a Sunderland fan and all of that, but regardless of any sentimental reasons I was one of the few players at the club to have at least played at Wembley before and just that little extra know how might have come in handy somewhere along the line seeing as we were massive underdogs against Liverpool.

At least Gary got in, which was something. John Kay was man enough to admit he was not fit enough to play and must have been even more upset than me to be missing out because he had been heavily involved in the run, but whilst it meant a reshuffle Gary was actually one of our better players on the day. Other than that though we didn't do ourselves any justice, after doing so much to help get us into the final John Bryne missed a half chance early on and we seemed to freeze.

Very few people felt let down though because the cup run had been brilliant and just as had been the case the year prior at Manchester City, the team had put their hearts into it. Sadly, one or two idiots didn't see it like that and blamed Gary for some reason so one night after the final he got a load of abuse outside his house in Fatfield. Owersy had actually got married that season however so soon after the cup final we all went and had a fortnight in Tenerife for his belated stag do, which was well over the top really.

Gary had married the ice skater Joanne Conway, who I would always call 'Frosty Arse' and I was his Best Man. The evening before he married Joanne, Gary and I went up to the top of Penshaw Monument to just take everything in and clear our heads ready for the big day, when we ended up having more than a few beers. Owersy had a few other family things going on during this time and I was really worried about him, but he would always be round either my Mam's house or at Gran's and Mam still calls him 'the devil' because we'd be getting under her feet or causing mischief - and she still says now that we were both wicked the day of that wedding, messing about all of the time. Just like Pratty, she loves Gary really though and has kept all of his footballing paraphernalia alongside mine.

We stayed in Wayne Lineker's apartment for the stag trip and the whole two weeks were mental; I didn't eat for a fortnight and came back like a stick because we were out every night, and for the second season in a row it was mainly because as a squad we were trying to forget about what had just happened to us. This time the lads had to get over losing to Liverpool, and from a personal point of view, I wanted to stop thinking about the season as a whole.

Another thing we did after going to Wembley was have a day at York Racecourse and I ended up going berserk at Crossa during the outing. It wasn't the most sensible thing I could have done and he ended up fining me, but I just didn't care because I was so devastated in the first place. I think I wanted to provoke him into giving me an explanation as to why I hadn't been in the team but that's how football is sometimes, and it had been and gone by that point so I wouldn't have got the answers I wanted anyway.

What people started to fear was that getting to the final papered over a few cracks in the side. Obviously players subconsciously kept back a bit in the later league games as they didn't want to miss out on a Wembley appearance and Crossa had to manage the squad as best he could to get us through the fixture pile up our run had caused, but even when you allow for that we were too far off the pace to still think the squad was good enough as a whole.

We still showed ability in fits and starts but after all the excitement of the last few seasons the club was now in a rut and we went into a real period of turmoil. I don't think there was enough joined up thinking between the board and the football management side of things and whilst other clubs were looking to get into the new Premiership we seemed to drift along on the pitch and got overtaken by others because behind the scenes nobody appeared to have an actual plan.

The season after the cup final was dreadful, and a second relegation back into what was now Division Two was a serious possibility. I had started the campaign with Crossa using me in midfield and for a while that looked like a route back into regular first team football but that too fizzled out and I was soon back in the same old cycle of injuries.

Bobby Ferguson had been brought in as an assistant to Malcolm over the summer and all he would do was talk about his Ipswich Town days. He was at the club during their successful period in the late 1970s and the early 1980s and it was Bobby that saw me in training and picked up on the fact that I could pass the ball and that it might be worth moving me back into midfield; I certainly hadn't gone to the manager saying that I had played there before, Bobby just spotted something and wanted to give it a go, and obviously I was more than happy to go along with that.

Bobby was a bit of an eccentric in truth and had his own ways; he swore like a trooper and would get up early and fight the waves on Whitburn beach just to get his rise. He could be quite funny in the way he did things too and would have this thing about 'visualising' what you wanted to do; even when we were up in Ayr for pre season and Gary and I were on the putting green he came over screaming at us, insisting that we had to shut our eyes before taking the shot because we'd been missing them all day, he was crackers.

He definitely fancied me as a midfielder however and would try to boost my confidence on a lot of occasions. He pushed my case a fair bit and brought Crossa round to his way of thinking and after being used in a sitting role against Ayr I was asked to carry it on into the early games of the season and did quite well. Although I was being used in a holding role and wasn't being asked primarily to attack I still got into a couple of good scoring opportunities by timing runs from deep and hit the post on a couple of occasions, and just to rub it in even more I picked up another niggle and was back out of the side just as I was hitting my stride.

Denis had tried me as a midfielder a couple of times in pre season games too and it had been hard to pick it back, even though I had played there so much as a youngster. When you start playing at the back you get used to everything happening in front of you, so when I got moved into midfield again under Crossa I had to remember to open my body out more and to try and spot what was happening around me. It was a little bit strange at first but I got there, and it was only after I had returned to fitness after picking up this daft injury that I kind of naturally fell back into being seen as a defender again as results and other injuries dictated.

To say I was left frustrated again was putting it mildly. It didn't matter who was in charge or what I did on the pitch, I couldn't get the breaks; the midfield experiment had been going well until my body let me down and after that I had another couple of runs in the side before again having to drop out through injury each time - and all the while we were yet again hovering around the bottom of the table.

At the end of November and the start of December it looked for a little while as if things were about to pick up. Gabbers was now at Derby County and we managed to beat them in awful conditions at the Baseball Ground before winning at Southend

United and then beating Barnsley at Roker thanks to goals from Sean Cunnington and Mickey Gray, who had replaced me at left back due to another minor injury to make his first senior start and scored within seconds of kick off. We were soon back in the mire however a week later when I was an unused substitute and Brentford came up and beat us, and after our game at Tranmere Rovers was called off in February and the Pools Panel awarded them a home win it was clear to everybody what a hole we were in and Crossa was sacked.

A few jokes did the rounds about how he was given his cards on the back of a defeat in a game that wasn't even played, but there was little option in truth. I have seen Crossa since and he is always the same jovial self but he was never cut out to be a manager really and I think he knows that himself. What might have made the situation a bit harder for him to stomach however was the fact that he loaded the gun himself as it were, and stepping into his shoes was Terry Butcher, a player Crossa had himself signed at the start of the season.

I had a lot of time for Butch, at first

CHAPTER TEN

Butcher and the boo boys

On the pitch Terry Butcher was one of the best in the business but during his time as manager at Sunderland he did not reach the same heights. Bobby Ferguson knew him very well following their time at Ipswich Town and he had a big hand in bringing him on board, and whilst we all knew that he could bring something to the club as a player a lot of people, and that includes some fans and some players alike to be honest, felt from the off that Crossa was mad to sign somebody that had already been a player manager at Coventry City and would possibly be seen as an obvious alternative should things go wrong.

Purely as a player, me and Butch got on great. We played together against Derby County to start that run of three games where we thought it was going to come good under Crossa and worked like a dream, even if the fanzine 'A Love Supreme' referred to us along the lines of the 'slowest centre half partnership the club have ever had!'. The match was played under pouring rain at the Baseball Ground and it stands out because Derby had been spending fortunes trying to get promoted. Gabbers was there and so too was Paul Kitson so I had a couple of personal battles going on, and at one point I looked up at the stands and half of Murton was there watching on.

The game shouldn't have been on really because the ball was holding up in the surface water, but Butch seemed to thrive in adversity. He was similar to me in style, but he was bigger than me and was very vocal so I learnt a lot from him on the communication side of the game. He made an effort to be part of the group too and even though he was a big name he had no problem joining in with the banter. Both as a player and as a member of the squad he was excellent, he would help bring others on in training and would come on nights out with us and have a drink on the bus back from away games, but when he took over from Malcolm he changed overnight I thought.

Few people would have been surprised when he replaced Crossa, it had been on the cards virtually since the day he arrived at the club after all, and we knew that he could no longer just act like one of the lads but the way he seemed to change at the click of a finger was a shock. He was such a strong leader on the pitch but perhaps being a former team mate made it harder for him than it would have been for somebody coming in new to the club, although it had worked elsewhere probably because they adapted gradually rather than switching in an instant.

It got a lot of people's back up as they didn't know where they stood anymore and the mood within the changing room meant it wasn't always a nice place to be anymore I felt. Maybe if Butch hadn't have been right under the club's nose Crossa might have hung around longer, but most people agreed something had to be done and this was another quick internal appointment; it just happened to be the wrong one for my mind.

It was proving to be another tricky period for the club and for me personally, the season was over with two months to go due to yet more injury problems. It was never a leg break or similar keeping me out though, where you could at least see the process through to the end and know that the problem was getting better, it was always a strain or a tear and I think if anything that was worse. At least I had been able to get a few more appearances under my belt that season and 1992-93 had been the first time since we consolidated in Division Two four years ago that I had played more than twenty times. That was some slight comfort for me but the change of manager didn't really have the desired effect on results long term however, as whilst we only lost one of Butch's first six games we then went on a shocking run and won only two of the remaining fifteen that campaign.

When people talk about those first few months under Butch the trip to Newcastle United always comes up. It was probably best that I was injured for this one because it has gone down in infamy; he took the rest of the squad back to Ayrshire for team bonding before the game and I've been told since that he turned up for breakfast one morning with all of his hair shaved off, telling the lads he wanted them to go into the derby like the SAS, get a result and get back out and all of this, and even as early as then people started thinking that Butch was starting to lose control.

People didn't trust him anymore and were unsettled so it is little wonder that results did not improve. We lost the Newcastle United match and in the end we were very lucky to stay up. We got beat 3-1 on the last day of the season at Notts County and only escaped relegation because of results around us and whilst I didn't play, I was in the changing room afterwards with everybody else to see Butch come in and launch the tea pot across the floor. We all expected him to then give us a speech or to have a go at us, but instead he just sat down and looked like he was sulking, I even wondered if he was crying. We needed something to lead us into the next season, a rallying call, but in the end we were just looking at each other thinking he was acting like a spoilt kid.

Butch was obviously thinking that we weren't good enough as a squad but the way he went about it was all wrong, it was just not the way to handle a group of people that needed rousing at all. Within a few days of the season ending he retired from playing and called in a load of players, Gary included, and told them he was going to move them on and that proved to be an error too, because of course none of them were sold in the end and they were left with everybody else knowing their manager didn't want them but still seeing them getting picked.

People were griping about him left right and centre but in football you have to be careful what you said; I don't know if the player's opinions ever got back to the chairman and if they did, what Bob Murray would do about it anyway? After all, he wouldn't sack a manager purely on the word of a player that might have their own agenda for instance and it didn't matter how close I felt we all were there might have been snitches within the changing room ready to go running to the manager.

Even if players are unhappy or think things aren't being done correctly they might not voice it too loudly just in case the wrong person overheard. I don't necessarily think it was the case in this instance but players brought into a club by the current manager for example might be more loyal to him than somebody that had arrived earlier and as is the case in all walks of life you just had to bite your tongue and get on with it.

Butch did of course bring in plenty of his own men. Bob felt before the 1993-94 season that this was the time to release funds and allow some serious spending but why he did it with Butch, who had no record in the transfer market, and not Smithy I will never know. One of the new faces, thankfully now minus the tash, was Andy Melville and we would soon hit it off. Unbeknown to ourselves at the time really, we helped bring some of the group back together as we would often go for a drink and encourage the rest to join us; and Mel always seemed to know the score.

Derek Ferguson was another of the big signings that came in during the spree but I think he would say it himself that he could have done better at Sunderland. He was a bit deep really as a character, but he was capable of being a good player and was similar to Bracewell in style; he could link the play up well but when we struggled as a team he found it hard to make an impact on the match.

Derek didn't get off to the best of starts when he crashed his car driving back from a pre season game. To make matters worse most of the other new arrivals were also in the car with him and although we didn't know it at the time he was trying to come to terms with some personal difficulties so he could have done without this extra problem. We were in the dark about this at the time though so just put it all down to home sickness after he moved from Scotland, but you could tell something was not right.

The move to Sunderland was meant to have been a fresh start for Fergy, and it was meant to be a fresh start for everybody else at the club too, but we started the season with a batch of unwanted old players, a batch of unavailable new players and to top it off, an unpopular manager. Our first game of the season was a disaster as well, we lost 5-0 at Derby, and whilst we again showed the odd glimpse, impressive wins such as when we did the double over Premiership side Leeds United in the League Cup were the exception rather than the norm.

From my point of view, at least I wasn't one of the group that was told they were on the unwanted list and I always thought that Butch rated me. In Crossa's second season and then under Butch I found I was starting to get back into the team on

WHO NEEDS CANTONA WHEN WE'VE GOT DICKIE ORD!

a more consistent basis, but with the club in a mess that in turn had lead to me becoming a real target of the boo boys. The situation had been growing since Crossa's time, and as odd as it seems I honestly think that me being a Sunderland fan had something to do with it.

When I was first coming through it hadn't really affected me, it was great to be doing something I had dreamt about as a boy but when I was playing I just focused on the game itself; there was no time to be getting misty eyed or self aware and it wasn't until after my problems with Smithy that I felt low on confidence and under pressure to perform. Sometimes though, my background meant that certain people in the crowd would single me out and felt that because I had followed the club I should have been able to do the impossible.

As a local lad all I wanted was to do well for the club but I started getting stick more and more. Under Butch I'd been permanently shifted to left back and with the team as a whole was struggling as much as ever, fans started openly booing me at games; it was horrendous. The one that really stands out for me when it comes to getting abuse was against Peterborough United early in Butch's reign, as even though we won I was getting stick from a group within the Clock Stand and I really was getting it in the neck.

There was a point during the game where I went on a run from left back, beat a couple of men and put in a perfect cross for Don Goodman; he couldn't miss really and it put us two ahead, and it was after that move that I was about to have a go back at this section before thinking better of it at the last moment.

I wasn't playing badly during this period necessarily, but the club was in turmoil and I think the fans needed to pick on somebody so with me being used out of my natural position I was an easy target. As a centre half you are working as a pairing and can see the game in front of you much better, but a full back you are one on one against the winger and you can get turned over. It was always in the back of my mind that somebody could knock the ball past you and get in behind and if you are not settled you will never produce your best. I never really had a nightmare where I thought I deserved to be dropped, and that season I was steady away, but there will always be an element within a home crowd that want to pick people out.

Don't get me wrong, this is something I think you get at all clubs and I truly feel that Sunderland have the best travelling fans around. At away games, even when we lost all the fans would applaud you and I would sometimes walk off thinking

'I can't even look at them' because I felt we had let them down, and in fairness probably 90% of the home fans at our games were magnificent too but some will have been getting hassle from the missus or something like that, and they then come out wanting to vent their frustrations and will do it at the match because it is easy, not realising the affect it can have on the team they are meant to be supporting.

My Dad has always known the game and sometimes he would have been watching a match and come away saying the same sort of things as me; the stuff some people shout out just shows how little they know; they will have a go at a player for being out of position for example when its not really the case, or turn up already with an opinion and only see the things they want to and when that is the case it doesn't matter what you do in the game they will have a moan.

The abuse wasn't just at games however. Shortly after the Peterborough match I got the injury that would keep me out of the side for the rest of the season, and people would come up to you just as much to have a go about you not being in the team as they would if you were playing badly. I remember once being in a restaurant in Seaburn called the Shagorika with all of the lads from Murton and their partners and this bloke just came up and started mouthing off. We were out for somebody's birthday so it upset her of course, and all the lads were sticking up for me, but in that position footballers just have to sit there and take it regardless.

It's awful how all the booing and hassle makes you feel, and I can't think of many other jobs you could do where that would happen so it is bound to have an impact on you in your personal life. Before this point my drinking had been a social thing in many ways, but now I had gone from a position when I was on a YTS and making my first appearances and alcohol didn't appeal at all to me then being at a point where I was in smaller groups or just drinking alone. Being frustrated and then off work on a Monday it was easy to have a drink and that in turn would lead to arguments and yes, it had a knock on effect and in my case caused problems at home too.

I'd met my fiancée Nicola through cricket when she was coming through to Murton with a mate that was seeing one of the other lads. We ended up together for seven years and it got really serious, but we split up during the previous season and it was mainly through the stress I was starting to feel; I had been unhappy when I was out of the side and yet now I was back in I was dreading the games.

99

Being a nervous individual anyway, all it made me do was want to go and lock myself away in the house or be by myself. That's what I would do up until the Saturday, then once the match was over I would feel the relief come over me so would go out on the drink and unwind. That was how I coped with it, but I knew that friends and family were feeling it all too and with them all being nearby they couldn't get away from it either. You live and learn however, and looking back I should have tried to do more to concentrate on the football. I let things get to me, but hand on heart I can say that I never, ever wanted to leave Sunderland and no matter how bad things got it didn't cross my mind once.

Slowly but surely, my situation started to improve and instead it was the manager packing his bags as Butch got the bullet having served less than a year in charge, in which time I had met, engaged and married my new wife Sonia. My ex Nicola was a lovely lass, she was a salt of the earth character but we were living together at a time I was going off the rails a little bit and it caused tension. I then met Sonia in the Village Inn one night; she was from Murton too yet I had never seen her before in my life, and with me being in a rut football wise I needed something else and we had a whirlwind romance. We went to Turkey the summer Butch was busy splashing the cash and were soon engaged, before getting married that November.

Things first started getting better for me on the pitch at the same time we were making plans for the wedding and it helped that I got two goals in fairly quick succession, the first of which was the best I ever scored. It was at home against Grimsby Town and it was important, because it came in the last 10 minutes and got us a 2-2 draw to take us off the bottom of the table. What made it even better for me was the fact that Grimsby had gone two ahead after one of my clearances had fallen to Nigel Jemson and his shot hit off Martin Gray for an own goal. Nicky had made his England Under 21 debut in the same game I had and I felt slightly responsible for the goal but after Don got us back into the game we began turning the screw.

It was another night game at Roker Park and just as we were starting to worry that time would run out before we made the break through I started carrying the ball forward towards the Fulwell End and from about 35 yards out heard Gordon screaming "shoot" so I put my head down, hit it, and looked up to see it bounce down off the bar. If I knew it had crossed the line I would have been off, but Phil Gray, Tippy, headed it into the net to be sure and I assumed it was his goal. It was only when we where running back for the restart and he told me it had already gone over the line that I knew it was actually mine, but by that point I didn't have time to do my usual routine and go berserk!

After making a full recovery following the injury problems at the end of the previous season I was starting to feel my way back towards some sort of confidence too and it helped that because of that goal the fans were now encouraging me to shoot every time I got the ball and were getting behind me a bit. The 4-1 defeat at Ayresome Park against Middlesbrough in October took us back into the relegation zone though and their first goal after seven minutes came when I was fouled in the build up.

I had to come off with concussion and was meant to be out for two weeks, but I actually came back the following weekend against West Bromwich Albion and it proved to be a major turning point in my career. To be fair to Butch we did seem to have a lot of injury problems as a squad that season and with us getting down to the bare bones I came back sooner than would normally be recommended, and the gamble proved worth it because I scored the only goal of the game.

This time it was another header; Martin Smith put the cross in from a free kick with about half an hour to go and I'd timed my run perfectly to get to the ball first. That was a tight game actually, but it was entertaining too and I was up and down the flank a lot so I ended up getting taken off late on with a spot of cramp and got a standing ovation from the crowd. One of my mate's would always put a tenner on me to score the first goal and I think I was 40-1 that day so as soon as we got into the lounge afterwards he bought all the team our drinks. It was one of the rare times his bet paid off, and to cap everything I even managed to get nine out of ten in the Echo ratings on the Monday!

People saw the fact that I was prepared to play so soon after taking a knock to the head and I think it made some of my detractors realise that I was doing everything I could for the cause after all. It always seemed to be the case that I would get injured again whenever things were going well though, and sure enough I then had to come off in the midweek League Cup defeat to Aston Villa because of a hamstring pull, but this time it felt slightly different because I'd made a breakthrough in terms of improving my reputation.

The West Brom win was the last victory under Butch, and starting with the Villa game we lost the next seven matches, the sixth of which was his last in charge and came a day before my wedding. The stag do for the squad before hand had been a mess; it was at Tall Trees nightclub in Yarm and the plan was we would all head down after our match on the Saturday against Portsmouth. The game was part of that losing streak so we were all drinking heavily on the bus down and from that point it got out of hand a touch.

It was meant to be an all weekend thing but some of the group were going back that night and as I was missing my lass I jumped on the mini bus to come home early, but I was that drunk it was only when I got in on the Monday for training that I found out what had gone on. I was in the big bath in the changing rooms and Butch came in and made some comment about a cow. I had no idea what he was on about so he told me "I've just had the Echo on the phone, he told me that Dickie Ord's stag party knocked a cow over on the A19 and it was killed" - I was on that bus and I didn't even know.

The story was covered on the local news and everything, so I soon found that the cow had somehow got loose and that the road had needed to be closed whilst it was all sorted out. I must have been asleep the whole time however and when I got to Murton I was in such a state that I was just lying in the garden before deciding that it was a good idea to ring for a taxi to take me straight back to the party.

My hamstring had recovered in time for the next game, but we were comfortably beaten at Tranmere Rovers before losing to Southend seven days later. That was 24 hours before the wedding and overnight it had started snowing; so it made for some great photos. The guy taking them was Ian Lawson, who is Gordon's brother in law, and there was a little story about us the following day in the Echo alongside a picture of me and Sonia with all of the squad.

Gary returned the favour to be my Best Man and the ceremony was at St Joseph's in Murton before having a great reception at Shotton Hall. Butch allowed me to have a couple of days off so Sonia and I went to Edinburgh for our honeymoon, but by the time I was back there was all sorts of speculation that he was on his way and all the lads were desperate to fill me in on what I had missed whilst I was away.

Seemingly the day after the wedding he took them for a run around Whitburn and along the sea front to work off some of the booze. When he got them back to Roker Park though he just turned around and said "right, off you go again lads" but instead a couple just hopped on the bus on the way back rather than run the whole way again; our form was shocking anyway, and now that he'd well and truly lost the dressing room that was it for Butch.

Mick Buxton took over on the Friday but was unable to do anything to stop us losing at home the following day against Nottingham Forest. After that however it was another case of the new manager syndrome kicking in and we won three and drew one of the next four; it seemed like a marriage made in heaven.

Mick was always happiest on the training ground

CHAPTER ELEVEN

End of the internal affair

It was no surprise to me that Butch went, and few people would have been shocked to find that he was replaced with another internal appointment either. Mick Buxton had been one of Butch's coaches; he was a nice bloke and he came in to take over; but whilst I can't claim to know what Mick felt, at the time I didn't even think he particularly wanted the job.

Mick was close to Bob Murray though and I think he took over just to try and help him out, because nobody else would have fancied it to be fair given the mess we where in. He already knew the players at least and results picked up at first, so much so that we finished the season fairly comfortably and could have even squeaked into the play off places had we not lost a couple of late home games.

Just finishing the 1993-94 season well away from danger was in itself quite an achievement at Sunderland though because it always seemed as if we went into the last few weeks with something riding on the games. This was a new position for the club to be in and all he had done was introduce a bit of organisation and make us a bit more solid, but he benefitted too from the likes of Martin Smith, Craig Russell and Mickey Gray finding their feet; all talented young lads that like me were desperate to do well for the club they had grown up supporting.

Daft as it might sound, before Mick we didn't really have team meetings. With him though we would gather in a room at our hotel before away games and he would get the marker board out and go through the opposition in detail; a lot of clubs do it now, but they perhaps have tailored it a bit more and keep it more straight forward now because after initially galvanising us things with Mick could get very boring I felt and we lost any spontaneity in the following season.

Mick had done some stuff with the FA and he was ahead of his time in some respects. He would get us in to do extra training sessions during the afternoons and that too was not something we were used too, but whilst we perhaps did need our routines changed after being in something of a comfort zone under previous regimes you need balance too and to know when and how, because we went from doing very little to now spending time going over and over the same things.

With him being from Sunderland people would have loved to see Mick take us further but his insistence on going into the smallest detail with everything meant that the mid table finish in his first season was the peak, and even then I think I ended up with more points than the team! These were disciplinary points though, because I was booked in his first game in charge and ended the season with 12 yellow cards.

Of those, only two were for dissent and the rest were for foul tackles. That sounds like I was now going about trying to do people but that was never the case, I just think I was becoming more involved in games as both my confidence and fitness improved and that once you get a couple of bookings other referee's start to pay you too much attention and prejudge some of your tackles. That Forest game when Mick took over was a good example of me trying to impose myself really, they were a good side and eventually won promotion but we gave them a decent game and I had a right battle against Steve Stone.

He was one of those that would be happy to give it back if you gave him any niggle and that game was perhaps the most enjoyable I had in terms of having an ongoing duel. We were giving each other plenty of stick but every time we clashed we just got up and had had a laugh and a joke about it and that is exactly how it should be. Even Steve himself said to me afterwards that he loved our tussle; during the game he would say something and I would come back at him but it was all just banter, and because those in the Clock Stand were now backing me up too and egging us on as well it is definitely one that stands out.

Another game I remember well from that period was when we went down to play Oxford United early in the New Year. We had already pulled well clear of the Division One relegation zone by this point but this was a game that I was particularly keen to do well in because Denis Smith had only recently taken over as manager at the Manor Ground and had brought Malcolm Crosby in as his assistant. Anton Rogan and John Bryne were both there too by this point and we won by the same 3-0 score line that they had beaten us by in Smithy's last game as our manager, so he must have been sick afterwards!

I wanted to show them both that I had been capable of being a good player all along and that I had started turning things round after the way I'd been left in the cold by them. I was beginning to find my way at last after all of the doubts I had under Smithy and carried that form into the match; Martin Smith had already put us two ahead and with 10 minutes to go I timed a 50-50 challenge well and won possession for Don Goodman to make it 3-0. I made my point I felt, and under Mick not only were the pockets of fans that had previously booed me started to lay off me a bit, but I was becoming a bit of a favourite in some quarters.

The final thing that swung it for me was a change to my game that came about after sitting down with Pratty and having a real heart to heart conversation. Pratty knew more than anybody what had been going on with the crowd and what it had been doing to me and he just came out with, and I remember it perfectly, "you just need to start tw*****g people". I didn't get him at first, so he said "what do Sunderland fans want, they want to see people get stuck in". Now, there was more to it than that of course but we spoke more and what he was telling me made sense so basically, I started putting myself about a bit more and it seemed to do the trick.

I had never minded a tackle, but I was more of a reader and was about positioning myself before danger started; yet when I then got more physical and was approaching things differently, being a bit more 'in the moment' perhaps, the cycle changed and fans took to me again. I wasn't going in to maim people or losing control and taking myself out of the game but I became more robust I would say, I used my strength and would get closer to forwards a lot sooner. You could feel the mood towards me change and with that I became more confident and found I could mix the two styles; I wasn't scared to make a mistake and that meant I was less likely too anyway, which is how the mind often works in these cases.

The increase in yellow cards this all brought was a slight down side, and once the season was over I had to go to Lancaster Gate for a disciplinary hearing, but to be fair to Mick he could see what was going on and the reasons for it. I knew where to stop so I wasn't getting myself sent off and costing the team in that respect and he was happy to just take a slap on the wrist and forget about it, and I think he understood that it was making me a better player so was willing to put up with the negative aspects it brought.

I think it was fair to say that the train journey and overnight stay with him in London before the hearing could hardly be described as a barrel of laughs but at least he was backing me up on this one. We turned up at Lancaster Gate the following morning and were put in front of this big table of about ten people in blazers. Half of them were falling asleep and to be honest it was embarrassing for them; they didn't know who we were and they all just seemed to be going through the motions so I ended up I think with a token fine, but it was worth it to an extent because the fans were now on my side and I was enjoying games again, which meant so much after the different issues I'd been having before Mick took over.

Hardening up my tackling and being a bit more physical helped turn the tide and my biggest problem now was explaining the fine to Sonia, because we had just bought our first house together and the cash would have gone towards doing it up. At this point my contract was soon going to be up as well, so Mick had me called into the referee's room at Roker Park to discuss a new deal. I didn't know why he wanted to do it in there, but when I walked in I found him sitting on the toilet with the door wide open and I couldn't concentrate on a word he was saying. In the end I just had to say to him "look, can we talk about it tomorrow in your office" and the next day when we were up there all he wanted to do was ask me about this new house and what the garden was like. We were sat there for half an hour just with him telling me how to get some of my flowers right, he didn't even mention football, and it was more like chatting to some old bloke down the pub than any high level contract negotiations.

Things like that made you realise that the club was backwards in some ways, people like Mick were honest enough but things always ended up being a struggle on the pitch during that whole period after relegation in 1991 and we just seemed content to bob along doing the bare minimum. John Featherstone was the Chairman for a period but apparently Bob Murray was the major shareholder and it seemed to me that he was still the one that called the shots.

It seemed for a while that things were going to change when Butch was in charge as he was given a bit of money to spend, and in truth some of the players he brought in were good buys. Mel, Tippy and Alec Chamberlain for example would all play a part in us getting promotion down the line but for every signing that came off however you could argue that there was a poor one too and with results not picking up initially I dare say Bob probably felt he'd had his fingers burnt and so we went back to watching the pennies.

Mick didn't have much money to spend and we started the 1994-95 season without any new blood coming in. Even though I had signed a new deal I heard rumours that Burnley and Millwall both approached the club about me and I know a call was made to Mick whilst we were away in Norway for a pre season tour, but whether any firm offers were made I don't know. It wasn't something I was looking at doing though and in fact it was Ian Sampson that left, so that at least meant less competition for me and in terms of arrivals it was only when Ian Snodin came up on loan from Everton a couple of months into the season that we saw a new face.

That was it until the end of November when Don was sold to Wolverhampton Wanderers and there was finally a bit of cash in the coffers, but in a round about way it actually lead to me being left out of the side again. We started the season well and didn't lose any of our first eight games, but because six of them finished as a draw we still weren't challenging at the top of the table and sure enough we soon started dropping further and further off the pace and by December were hanging around just above the relegation places yet again.

My own situation had improved ten fold but as a professional in a team sport you cannot look out for just yourself, and that thing of being a Sunderland fan meant I was as desperate as ever for us to do well. I wanted to be in the side, but it was just as important that we were winning so even though I was a first team regular at last to say I was happy would be pushing it. My body had developed enough so that I was getting away from constantly picking up niggles though, and it was a good feeling to be able to play and train freely without the possibility of breaking down hanging over me.

I wasn't invincible however, and the season had started with more woe; just this was at least as a result of a 'proper' football injury. I took a knock to my knee in the final warm up match of pre season when we where at home to Sheffield Wednesday and had to come off after half an hour, but just as I was starting to worry that it was going to be another hard luck story we found that it was nothing too serious thankfully and within a couple of weeks I was back in the fold and was then brought into the side against Wolves to start a run of 19 consecutive starts, which was easiest my longest run in the starting eleven.

It is a statistic that underlines the problems I had been having trying to establish myself before then, but at 24 I was no longer just a young kid happy to get a game here or there and I was finally becoming less of a bit part player and feeling more like I belonged, which is of course when I got another kick in the teeth. Now I was settled in the side it was always going to hurt were I ever to be dropped, and when the run did come to an end it was done in such an embarrassing way that it was a bigger blow than ever before.

As Mick had got hold of some money he went back to Bristol City to try and bring Martin Scott to the club; he had gone after him in the summer too and was now upping his bid, but they turned down a cash only deal and instead asked for a player plus cash offer including Owersy, who was being used on the right wing at the time. They probably wanted to see if Gary could do a job at full back before they went ahead with a swap deal and sure enough, when they came to Roker Park the following Saturday Gary got moved to left back, which is where I had been playing - just nobody bothered to tell me.

We had lost at Millwall the previous week and although it had been a shocking performance there was nothing to suggest I would be picked out and nobody said anything different to me during the week so in I came and started to get ready as normal. I used to get changed in the little weights room to the side of the changing room a lot then, I could hang my clothes there but it was more out of habit than anything else really, and so I was ready with all my kit on in time for the warm up when Benno started laughing and asked me if I had seen the team sheet.

At that point Mick came in and asked to have a word with me in the groundsman's room where he told me that I was being dropped; I was foaming about how long he'd left it before telling me and ended up having a bit of a go at him before getting up and booting a hole in the door and storming off to get changed again.

None of the other lads could even look me in the eye before the game and the way it was done was all wrong. Obviously, if he had told me the day before I'd not have felt such an idiot in front of the lads and getting the man management side of things is so important, as I had found to my cost when I was first dropped under Smithy. Football was still old school then though and players didn't have the power they seem to have now; we were used in some ways and you were expected to just do as you were told and be a good boy.

Most of the time Mick was an honest bloke though and I don't think he liked having to make decisions or upsetting people. He even apologised to me afterwards because he knew it had made me look stupid, but I was still upset because of that and the fact Gary was leaving. It upset him too, we had been close ever since our days in the hostel and I don't think he ever wanted to leave. He wasn't just a big loss to me though, the rest of the lads loved him too and he was often at the centre of the social side of things. You know that people will be forever moving about in football, but Gary and I had grown up together in many respects and his departure was harder to take than most. Alongside Pratty he is my best mate and we still keep in close touch to this day, despite the fact that he has lived down in the west of the country ever since.

I must say that bringing Scotty in was a good bit of business because he proved to be a quality player, but now he was at the club he became the first choice left back and I had to sit out on the sidelines again. Even at a club like Sunderland though where the group was so closely knit there is a hidden rivalry between players, although nothing is ever said. You know who is in your position and you want to replace them or keep them out of the team, but rather than cause rifts it just helped make sure that people were always on their toes and if ever I was out of the team it would never be the case that I was hoping other lads would play badly or that we would lose so that I would come back into contention.

Throughout virtually all my time in fact the spirit amongst the players was fantastic and it would be very rare for there to be a real fall out. In the main people seemed to get on with everybody else as much as could be expected given the nature of the job and the only real ongoing problem that I ever remember there being within the camp was still rumbling on during this point in time. We came in from training one morning to find Derek Ferguson having a big barney with Darius Kubicki and everybody had to rush in the split them up, nobody was ever sure what started it but I felt the pair of them allowed it to fester and would blank each other from then on.

I remember it so well though because it was usual, there would be bust ups on occasion of course but normally people would be keen to kiss and make as soon as possible. Other than those instances, Sunderland had a really strong dressing room pretty much throughout my time at the club and even in adversity we stuck together as a group of players. Compared to other clubs I always thought we got on like a big family and the worst you would ever get would be a bit of bickering, and before he left it would usually be Marco Gabbiadini to blame! I know him and Owersy in particular had their moments with each other, but Gabbers would always be brought down back to earth by the rest of us before too long.

I think the reason we managed to stay so close was because there wasn't any superstars allowed in the dressing room, although you might argue that was simply because we weren't good enough! To be fair to him, Marco probably was the closet we got to a star though, certainly until Reidy came, and he was the best I had played with at that point. All it was with him was that he fancied himself a bit, he is sound now though and I must say he comes across very well now he is in broadcasting.

It took about two months before I was back in the side. I didn't ever really see myself as an outright full back and my versatility did me some good because I was able to come back in at centre half when a space opened up. I felt too at this point as if I got myself into a position where if I impressed enough in training I could force my way back into the manager's plans as opposed to being merely a stop gap, and I knew I was dependable enough to keep my place once I got in.

Mick's influence was stifling the team though and we were edging closer to the relegation zone. He knew his stuff; he just couldn't get it across properly. As he was left footed as well it would always be Martin Smith that seemed to cop it, Mick was constantly showing him how to do things even though Martin had a wand for a foot. In my mind, training was boring and we were becoming boring to watch, which people could at least accept had we have been managing to get results, but that wasn't the case either.

Things started reaching breaking point in March when we played Stoke City at home and during the game the fans waved red cards in protest at the way the club was going. As it happens, we won that game thanks to a goal from Mel but it was only a temporary reprieve as we lost the next four, the last of which was at Barnsley in what proved the final straw. Brett Angell made his debut and had a goal disallowed, but it was Dominic Matteo that caused the stir because he wasn't registered correctly when he came on loan from Liverpool and there was a big chance that the FA would dock us some points as a result.

Dominic would have been a decent singing had the club not messed it up and we were grateful to only end up with a fine. The game itself should have been called off anyway though, we played in gale force winds and of course everybody that was there remembers that Barnsley were building a new stand at Oakwell and all of the dust and grit from the site was being blown into the away section.

It wasn't affecting the players but none of the Sunderland fans could see anything because it was flying into their eyes, which was probably a good thing to be fair because we were desperate. The match finished 2-0 so even without a points deduction we were too close to the relegation zone for comfort and that was it for Buxton. We were together as a squad but the mood in and around the club was desperately low and he needed to go; he could have perhaps gone sooner really, but the way things first worked out under his successor couldn't have been any better for the club or myself.

I don't think there was any real ambition before the end of the 1994-95 season and the club got left behind when the Premiership and all of its trappings kicked in. During the early to middle part of the decade we just seemed to be at a standstill, Bob looked happy for managers to carry on doing what they were doing but didn't have the conviction to give them money to spend and even when Smithy got us promoted he only gave him a few hundred thousand, which was nowt. We seemed to go through a cycle of sacking somebody, doing enough to stay up under the new guy and then falling away again, but I think that the red card protest and the embarrassment over Matteo were both wake up calls and he started paying more attention to things.

Instead of giving the job to another member of the current staff Bob's new appointment was external, and he breathed new life into the club. Suddenly, the next few years saw big changes and the club is unrecognisable now to the Sunderland of the mid 1990s. My career went forward too; I was already getting there under Mick but even then didn't realise what I had in me; like the club as a whole, four different managers had taken me on and none of them used me to my potential or had got to the bottom of my malaise.

In football it was just a case of you are in the side or you are not, most managers would not come and put an arm around you, even if you were the victim of abuse from the crowd, or tell you why they made their decisions. Their door would always be open, but I was never one to go in and cause trouble so I just had to get on with things and the odd time I did react it was through sheer frustration and I did it in the wrong way.

Things soon changed however. Professional managers are to an extent all at a fairly similar level when it comes to tactics and coaching; what sets them apart is how they treat the players that they have at their disposal and there was no better example of this than in 1995-96. Peter Reid was now at the club and the impact was startling. Within a season Sunderland were in the Premiership.

Every player wants that badge on their sleeve

CHAPTER TWELVE

Premier Passions, Episode One

Come the Premier League season I was flying, as under Reidy I had come on leaps and bounds and was on top of my game. Everybody was buzzing actually, and so it was to Ireland again for pre season, where as had been the case the year before as long as you were doing the business in training and in the warm up games and you weren't abusing the trust you were allowed out on a night and to mingle with the fans.

I was coming off the back of a promotion and testimonial year and couldn't wait for the season to begin. Being in the Premiership meant so much to everybody, and all of those little things that perhaps get taken for granted nowadays were all new to us, like being given our own squad numbers. We had used them for a couple of seasons in Division One before dropping them again, but now being given a Premiership squad number felt special somehow, as there was a bit of prestige to it.

When I first came into the game it was still the case that your position on the pitch dictated what number you would wear and so when we first had squad numbers I was given the number three as I was being used primarily as a left back. Our names were on the back of our shirts for the first time too and I remember playing Millwall at The New Den and going to the touchline to take a throw in, where all I could hear was this bloke screaming "Ord?, ORD?? What type of name is that you stupid ****?", so after that I refused to take any more throw ins!

Then, even though players were no longer required to wear them, Bally had made a thing of playing in the number five shirt during the promotion season even though he was playing in centre midfield and I somehow ended up playing with a number eight on my back as a result. It was one of those odd things where I then happened to have a couple of good games anyway though, so I wanted to stick with it and come the Premiership I asked the gaffer for it and the number eight has been my favourite number ever since; it's my lucky number I suppose and I've even got it on my personalised car registration plate.

As well as new squad numbers the club brought out new kits for that season. With it being the last season at Roker Park they were quite traditional and I liked them personally, but the manufacturers were still a local firm called Avec and some of the lads had a bit of a gripe about it because they didn't want to be seen as paupers and all of this. Everybody wanted to be wearing gear by companies like Nike or what have you but I doubt the club had those types of options available to them to be fair; I can't say it made that much difference to what I could produce on the pitch anyway, but a lot of footballers are posers and maybe it is another one of those mind tricks like having a particular squad number.

One thing I was fussy on during this period of my career was the type of boot I wore; they had to be Adidas World Cup's and nothing else. A year or so before I think, Reebok set up an office in Sunderland down by the river and I was approached to see if I was willing to switch. There wasn't any money involved but I got some gear for me and the family so I was happy to go along with it until I actually got them and tried them a couple of times. I just couldn't get away with them for some reason so I went round to a cobblers near Roker Park and got him to put the Reebok logos onto my old pair; I've never told them to this day but honestly, I hated those boots!

The World Cup boots suited me perfectly, and again, physiologically I felt better wearing them. They were good boots too though; they fit comfortably. I always had a decent first touch but if I wore anything with thicker leather it wouldn't happen so carrying on with a different brand wouldn't have been worth it.

In the build up to the new season there was, as you expect, all sorts of speculation about Reidy signing this player or that player. He made a point however just a few days before our first game of coming out in the papers and talking me and Mel up, which made us both feel great. I don't know, maybe he was working behind the scenes to try and bring somebody else in but to read of him saying that he felt we would have more than enough to cope in the top flight was another little masterstroke, we were confident in each others ability anyway and at that point I was more settled in myself than I had ever been so this just topped it up even more. Mentally and physically I was right there so I was looking forward to the season as a whole and seeing what the Premiership was going to be like; and you could say the same for the rest of the lads too.

Two days before the season kicked off, Reidy did bring somebody in - but he wasn't a defender. Instead, our new record signing was a man that would go on to play one of the most important roles in Sunderland's modern history both on and off the pitch. Niall Quinn was already a big name within the game and I had played against him when we were last in the top flight and he was at Manchester City, but he would go on to become a legend at Sunderland. He was a lot like Mel really, a bit quiet in some regards but from the off you could tell he had a very dry sense of humour and once he'd had a drink he was a great laugh.

I would soon get to know Quinny well but the season started exactly as it had done the year before, at home to Leicester City. We were up against a young Emile Heskey and he outpaced me and Mel a few times, which wasn't the hardest thing to do in all honestly, but we had picked up where we had left off the previous year as a partnership and the team got a point, which was an improvement on the game in their previous visit when we lost. Then it was off to Nottingham Forest, and my first trip rooming with the Big Man.

I could get nervous when I met new people and would go into my shell, so when he came into our hotel room and said he wanted to go to sleep I was happy enough. I wanted to catch up on the cricket scores on Teletext though, so then suddenly I was making all of this noise and he didn't know what was going on! Quinny tells the story better but after that I think he just went downstairs to kill time, and he has since told our mate Aidy that it was the longest telephone conversation he ever had with his missus because he was bored to tears being in with me!

I soon found out however that you had to be a secretary when you shared a room with Quinny, because he had that many contacts and newspaper columns and whatever, and every time he went out of the room it seemed his phone would start ringing again. He had the first mobile phone I ever saw in my life and it was massive, he brought it on the team bus on the way down to Nottingham and was playing cards with Sacko when the coach shuddered and it fell off the table onto his toe. The thing was like a brick and Sacko was jumping up and down calling him all sorts, it was hilarious.

It often happens that when a club comes up a division and already has a winning habit that they start quite well and get on a bit of a roll. We got to the City Ground then and got stuck into them right from the start and Mickey Gray gave us an early lead. Quinny got his first two for the club and with five minutes of the first half still to go we were 3-1 up, when we got a corner and I scored; it was Scotty that took it and I rose above Colin Cooper I think to rifle the ball into the net. The next thing I knew Paul Stewart and Niall Quinn were climbing on top of me celebrating but Mam and Dad weren't quite as happy because they only arrived at the ground during half time because of traffic problems so had missed my goal!

We went in at the break 4-1 ahead but as this was still August it was sweltering hot even though it was an evening game so Reidy told us to sit back a little bit and let them come at us; it wasn't really our style but we took it on board, slowed it down and finished the game looking a cut above them.

That proved to be out biggest winning margin all season however and it was the most goals we scored in a game too that campaign. Mel and I worked together like a dream at the back and we were solid for pretty much the whole campaign, but we soon started to find goals harder to come by and it would cost us points regularly. We went to Anfield next, and that was a good example; I was up against people like Stan Collymore and Robbie Fowler, which was exactly the type of challenge I wanted, but at the other end we just couldn't make our chances count.

Bally was put on my former England Under 21 colleague Steve McManaman and he didn't allow him a kick, and in fact we barely gave Liverpool a sniff all game. The game ended as another draw though when we should have won it really; I remember playing a diagonal ball to put Quinny through and we had a few other chances but we couldn't put them away and that proved to be the case on more than one occasion.

The game against Newcastle United at Roker Park was the first we lost that season, and of course we couldn't have picked a worse team. Despite being at Sunderland for so long this was the first time I was going to be play against them for the first team and I was that hyped up before hand that I was doing press ups and all sorts to try and use up some of the nervous energy. Mel thought I had lost the plot and kept asking why I was being like that, but even though I didn't grow up hating the Mags the way some people do I knew how much it would mean to everybody if we beat them and was getting caught up in the frenzy around the game; you could feel it in the build up around the place.

There was the rivalry in Murton and for some people that went over to proper hatred but I honestly was happy for Newcastle to do well as long as it wasn't at our expense. I wanted to beat them obviously and knew how it could lift the mood around the club but the edgier side of things wasn't something I liked to get caught up with. I still have that attitude even now; when it is Sunderland versus Newcastle I am desperate that we win but other than that it doesnt bother me personally in the way it does others.

Community really does mean a lot to me and football is massive part of a lot of people's lives in the North East and when you see proper clubs, local clubs, like Darlington struggle financially I really am upset by it. People put a lot of hard work into their clubs and I want to see them do well; I want people to be happy and to get on with each other, I know that is perhaps old fashioned and not how it always works out, but I really do. Its better for the area if everybody is doing well, thats how I see it anyway, and for me personally the Middlesbrough games always seemed to have something extra attached to them as opposed the Newcastle one, probably because I could have ended up there instead as a kid, but even then it's not that I dislike them.

You could sense however that there was real hatred in the air as the match started, even though away fans had been banned from the ground. It was a horrible atmosphere to play football in and I was told afterwards that one lad I know threw his lighter at David Ginola and then had the cheek to ask the steward to go onto the pitch and get it back for him! It was one of those where you shouldn't laugh really, but it was no surprise because a couple of that group could be a bit naughty and it wasn't unusual for them to get into some sort of scrape. I remember playing one game at left back for instance and having to dribble past one of them as I ran up the touchline because he had dragged some other bloke onto the pitch and was

118

punching him, and the worst thing about it was that they used to get their tickets through a policeman they knew, yet still went looking for bother.

We really went at Newcastle and controlled the game in the early stages before going ahead when Martin Scott scored with an inch perfect penalty. We then went really close when Stewy had an overhead kick and had that gone in I think we would have had enough to win because honestly, they seemed to only have two chances all game and won it, their finishing was that devastating. People always say that is what makes the difference in the top division but it is only when you see it first hand that you realise how good some strikers are; you can be looking at somebody thinking their is no danger and suddenly its in the net in the blink of an eye.

I felt as if me and Mel had Les Ferdinand and Alan Shearer in our pockets but our goalkeeper Tony Coton was playing through the pain barrier because he was injured and I think because it was in the back of my mind it lead to one of their goals. Tony had been another one of Reidy's big name singings and he had all the experience in the world, but he could barely walk he was in that much pain so when the ball came across me and I had the opportunity to pass it back to him I knew he was in trouble and I dallied instead. I also knew that Shearer was behind me so I couldn't play it the way I would have preferred to and instead of whacking it clear I ended up giving away a corner, which of course they then scored from.

I had a hell of a game and it was probably the one mistake I made all match, but I paid for it. The nature of the sport means you make countless little slips during the ninety minutes or do something you wouldn't normally like to but it's only when it costs a goal that you remember it and to do it in such an important game, where we could have won, only made it worse. Even Shearer felt they had been a bit fortunate to win, I still knew him through our time together with the England Under 21s in Toulon, and he made a point of saying to me afterwards in the players lounge that he didn't feel they deserved the win.

The lounge area of Roker Park wasn't the biggest so it was quite intimate, but even when it was a derby the players would in the main get on with each other once the match was finished and Newcastle's squad were no different to be fair. It really was the case that if people had a bit of bother on the pitch it would usually end with a handshake and a pint in the bar because you would both know it was just the competitive spirit making you be that way, and that's how it should be. Players should want to win, that is what fans want too of course, but they should also know where to draw a line under it and even after the derby that was the case.

I used to bring my family and friends into the lounge too and so did a couple of the other lads because back then they felt able to talk to the players from both sides. That contact is not available to even them now however because of the way players are sometimes seen; people are put on a pedestal and the game suffers because of it, I really do think that. It's wrong that fans cannot associate with the players at the top level and some players even go as far as thinking they are Gods. Obviously, when I was growing up I used to think that they were because they would be out on the pitch doing things you dreamt of, but as you get older you realise they are people like everybody else and whilst they deserve respect for the efforts they put in they are not better than anybody else in other respects.

Even after losing to Newcastle things went okay for the team up until well into the new year, but the West Ham United game a couple of days later gave further evidence of where our problems would lie. The match was our first to be shown live on Sky but we could only draw 0-0 despite Quinny having another good chance. Like TC, he wasn't fully fit really and some of the fans got on his back at that point because they didn't know that he was playing whilst carrying an injury. He ended up making things worse for himself because he got a more serious injury in our next home game against Coventry City and spent pretty much the rest of the season being out of action.

Being unable to score regularly was what did us in the end and I have no doubt that had Quinny been fit for the majority of our games we would have stayed up, because he later proved in a Sunderland shirt what a good player he is. Reidy had spent a large proportion of his transfer kitty getting Niall in though and with the money now gone there wasn't the back up. We were solid defensively in the main and if we got a lead we knew how to hold onto it, but we didn't get that first goal often enough and that was down to Quinny not being there.

In between those games against West Ham and Coventry we had a trip down to Derby County. They had finished as runners up to us the previous season so were also finding their feet in the Premier League; I had had a couple of memorable trips at the Baseball Ground for one reason or another and sadly this was to be the case yet again. The place was very outdated and in the away team dressing rooms there was only the one urinal and the one cubicle. It is unpleasant I know but shortly before kick off I was desperate to use the cubicle but because somebody was already in and I didn't want to miss the team talk and have Reidy lose it with me I had to use the urinal at short notice. I snuck back in when Reidy started talking, thinking that nobody would notice, but instead Sacko followed me and when he saw what

I had been forced to leave he started playing war. He even got a piece of cardboard to scoop it up with and started waving it around, but whilst all of the other lads were falling over themselves laughing Reidy didn't take too kindly to it at all and I ended up getting my ticking off anyway.

As for the game itself, I was against Gabbers again and he was doing his usual trick of backing into me to make it look like I was climbing over him. The referee kept falling for it and giving free kicks against me, and Gabbers was laughing his head off. David Elleray was in charge and I'd never found him to be a good ref at the best of times, but eventually he booked me for another supposed foul and I said to him "just look next time, see what he is doing"; but sure enough, it happened again a few moments later and he pulled me up so out of sheer frustration I groaned something like "you stupid b***ard" and that was it, I was given a second yellow and I was off with about an hour still to play.

Even Gabbers stuck up for me because others had been calling the ref much worse during the game than I had; but that was it as far as Elleray was concerned, you are never going to win the argument in that position and I was given the first red card of my career. I went for the dreaded early bath and watched the rest of the game from the side; it was a red hot day and we held on for most of the match but we gave away a late penalty and it was put right into the corner by Aljosa Asanovic to mean we lost by the one goal.

What was odd about that game was that Reidy had dropped Darius Kubicki without any warning and it meant he missed out on the club's consecutive appearance record. We had kept faith with the same back four that had done so well as a unit up to that point, but after that we had to cope with a few changes; Gareth Hall would often be put in at right back instead of Darius, and when Scotty got a serious injury soon after we had to make do without him too and he was that good a player he was perhaps as big a miss as Quinny.

Next up was a trip to Watford for a League Cup match and whilst in my hotel room I heard that familiar sound of Bally knocking on my door, and when I answered he told me to go and see Reidy immediately. I assumed I was in bother because of the sending off and when he just opened with "I'm fining you" I wanted him to know I was taking it on the chin and replied "I know, I know, I've let you all down; honestly gaffer, I'm gutted". Instead of agreeing though he just looked a bit puzzled for a moment before saying "oh, no Dickie; I'm not fining you because you got sent off, I'm fining because you had a crap and it ruined my team talk".

121

Sacko was in there as well and sure enough him and Bally started howling with laughter. I could see the funny side and it was good way of going about things; Reidy knew I would be upset because of the sending off and it was his way of teaching me a lesson perhaps but without going too far the other way. He did it a couple of times with people, if you were a little bit out of line you'd have to pay up for a meal for the rest of the lads or something like that, and he wouldn't make a massive thing of it unless you really messed up.

I was suspended for our trip to Highbury to play Arsenal but was straight back into the team for our next derby, when Middlesbrough came up. They took the lead but Alex Rae scored soon after with a first half penalty, it was a very tight game and I was having a right battle with Fabrizio Ravanelli. He was a typical goal scorer; he was just a poacher in the box and was fouling me all of the time but Boro had some quality names in their team and Graham Poll, who was the referee that night, I felt was too busy laughing and joking on with all of these foreign stars and trying to be their best mate that he wasn't paying the blind bit of notice to all of the shirt pulling and that.

Boro were given a dubious corner ten minutes or so into the second half and TC had to make a low save to give away another one, but this time it came in and there was all sorts of pushing and shoving going on in the box when all of a sudden Ravanelli was free to put it in from a couple of yards. I was going berserk with the ref because two or three of us had been fouled yet all he was doing was laughing at me; I was furious. A couple of minutes later, Nick Barmby got the ball just inside our half about a yard in front of me and we tangled. I was still fuming with this ref and I think the red mist came down, I went to stamp on his head but in the same split second I realised what I was doing so pulled back and didn't even touch him. The initial movement was there though and I was sent off again.

The game was another live on Sky job and I knew I had let everybody down so I was sat in the dressing room on my own in tears. I was distraught; I had been playing out of my skin before then, and then I'd gone and done this, or well really, done nothing, but I'd allowed myself to get worked up into a situation and had cost the side twice in such a short space of time. Reidy came in afterwards and was about to go crackers with me, but he saw that I was crying and pulled it back a bit; there was no point in him telling me because he could see that I knew it already.

Bally had a magnificent game though and got me out of jail a little bit because three minutes after I was sent off he set up Craig Russell for our equaliser and we managed a 2-2 draw. I still wasn't happy with myself however so afterwards I went down to a little restaurant by the riverside in the hope of getting out of everybody's way, but a couple of other Sunderland fans were in there and they ended up trying to cheer me up instead. It was my second red card in exactly a month; my only two in my entire career actually, and the timing was awful because my form had been such that I was being linked with a call up to the senior England squad.

I'd had a great start to the season and found that Reidy had been right as I was more than able to manage with the step up. I was getting a bit of national attention in the media and I was supposed to be going to this that or the other club according to the papers and then suddenly all the talk of a senior England call up started to surface. Journalists were referring to me as one of the best centre backs in the country and were saying things about how I was a certainty for a call up so I was trying to keep a level head about it all, but then came the Middlesbrough game when things all went wrong.

I was given an automatic three match ban for violent conduct plus an additional game because I had already been sent off and for once it seemed that my absence from the team was all of my own making, and I know Reidy was more disappointed than he let on because he too had touted me for an international call up. He had got Sam Allardyce in doing a bit of scouting for us so asked him to do a little extra and come in and just run me into the ground for a month whilst I was unavailable. I would train with the rest of the lads as normal and after that Sam would come along and put more work on for me. At that point I was in great shape anyway but it was as much about teaching me as anything else.

I was focused again and returned to the team as soon as my ban was up. I was a genuine first team regular and had been for a couple of years now, and whilst I knew I couldn't get complacent it was a good feeling all the same to be playing in the Premiership and giving a good account of myself in the main given my past struggles.

After my return, two games stand out for differing reasons; one I will never be allowed to forget and one that brought my last goal for the club. The first match was our trip to Old Trafford and unfortunately we came up against Eric Cantona at his best. I'd played there the year before in the FA Cup and also when we were last in the top flight under Smithy but this time was something else, as if Cantona now had a proper aura around him. He played in between the forward line and the midfield and it was always one of them; do you go and mark him and allow space behind or do you drop off?

123

If you do drop off he can just get his head up and do what he wants and he was probably the first player that I played against that did that. Cantona's skills spoke for themselves but what people didn't always realise was that he was a big strong lad too and you would bounce off him when you went for a tackle. There were three in my career in fact that would drop into that area between the two; Cantona, Teddy Sheringham and Dennis Bergkamp and they were the best three that I ever played against.

All the great players are arrogant, none more so than Cantona and of course everybody remembers his solo goal during that game; even now some of the lads take the mick out of me over it and whenever it is shown on the TV somebody will always text me about it saying 'you're on again' and I know instantly what they are on about. Its probably the goal I am best recognised for and it wasn't even mine; me and Mel bumped into each other and I must have tried to play offside about three times I think before he got into the box and chipped Lionel Perez, after which he turned round and put his collar up for one of the most famous moments in the history of the Premier League. I blame Bally for the goal though; earlier on he'd said to me "right, we are going to nail this fella" and if you look back at the footage we both have a swipe at him and get nowhere near, so basically it was his fault!

At least the next game, and again Derby were the opponents, saw me score a goal of my own. It was on Boxing Day and after losing heavily to Manchester United we were so fired up it was unreal; Bally was up against his old Portsmouth team mate Darryl Powell and they had a right old scrap, he'd needed to get a lot of treatment on the side of the pitch after Powell had wiped him out early on and it bubbled away after that and turned into an edgy game. We then got a corner with less than 20 minutes left to play and when Martin Smith curled it in I got my head on in it at the near post to put us ahead; their keeper Russell Hoult managed to get a glove on it but I had connected powerfully enough for it to go in and it was what you might say was a 'classic' goal from me seeing as it was another set piece header.

Craig scored another to make sure of the win and that was almost it for 1996, a year in which I had played in a championship winning side, enjoyed a testimonial and made a bit of a name for myself in the world wide attraction that is the Premier League.

There had been plenty of parties on the way of course, but it was the final one, the club Christmas Party, that topped the lot. For a start, it was fancy dress and because they couldn't remember the name of the place we were meant to be starting in, you had Quinny dressed as a monk and TC dressed as Long John Silver going from pub to pub in Seaham and Murton trying to find us.

Some of the places in Murton and Seaham became the players' favourite haunts and Murton it seemed would get the blame for everything, there was even one time when Alex Rae's wife turned up in The Colliery Inn asking everybody where he was hiding; but at that point he had never been anywhere near the place! The Colliery was one of those pubs where if ever you needed an alibi you could say you had been in there and the regulars would back you up. Nobody in there would ever say anything to drop you in it, but it meant that when Quinny and TC got desperate and asked for me they got told to clear off!

They eventually caught up with us and we all had a fine time on the beer before heading into Sunderland at about eight or nine o'clock. We all piled into Idol's but then from nowhere this bloke just came up to me and lamped me right in the face. Honestly, I was just stood there doing nothing when it happened and then all of a sudden everybody steamed outside for a massive brawl with this bloke and his mates, there was hell on; but of course we were all in fancy dress so looked a right clip.

Come the Monday morning then and Reidy was in a right mood; he called us all in and started having a go at us because the police had been on the phone to him. They had studied the CCTV footage and apparently you could see all sorts; TC had broken his leg in three places down at Southampton so was pushing people away with his crutches whilst one of the other lads, who had dressed as a woman, was battering some fella over the head with his handbag in the background for example and it all ended when Lee Howey came running into shot to save the day whilst dressed as Batman!

Reidy certainly wasn't impressed but it turned out that no charges would be pressed, probably because everybody down at the station had had such a good laugh looking at the tapes by the sounds of it. A little while later we found out by sheer coincidence that the lads we were fighting were all players at Durham City; one of them had taken a dislike to me for some reason so decided to have a pop, but at the time we had no idea who they were and those involved were long gone by the time I arrived at Durham down the line, although it is funny how things works out.

The squad at that time was probably as close knit as ever before, but whilst Reidy certainly didn't mind the drinking culture I do know that at some points he was worried about it getting a little bit out of hand. The Village Inn in Murton would be a regular venue for us on Sunday afternoons for example, we liked the Shakespeare Tavern in Durham and there was a place at Wreckington that a lot of the lads would go to on a Tuesday afternoon too; and Fino's in Sunderland was always popular if anybody was out for a late night. Mel and I would always be in the Seaton Lane Inn with Aidy and this was of particular concern to Reidy, and Sacko has told us since that he even went as far as sending Quinny of all people to investigate! Sure enough though he just ended up on the drink with us, and he can supp without a doubt. He manages to keep himself right though, but just what Reidy got from it in the end I don't know.

I do feel that we would rein it in when we needed too, although I must admit that in January I came a little close. That was when I had just signed the best contract of my life, one that should have set me up brilliantly for years to come, but sadly 1997 was when the party started coming to an end.

CHAPTER THIRTEEN

Premier Passions, Episode Two

I had become that reliable a player during Reidy's time in charge that by the New Year he was keen to pin me down on a new long term contract. I certainly wasn't looking to leave, but there were always rumours doing the rounds that other clubs were interested in me now and at 26 I was coming towards my prime, so it was something we had been discussing for a short while before tying up the day before we played Arsenal ar Roker Park.

In my early days we would do our own contract negotiations and I might have asked for a tenner or so more a week when my deals were being redone. I was never one to be pushing myself on the manager or making demands and the way Reidy liked to do things were just as casual I think. He was fair in that he would pay people what he thought they were worth and after we had got everything signed and sealed he offered me a drink.

When Reidy had arrived he'd got his secretary to put two fridges in his office; one packed full of bottles of Budweiser and one packed full of bottles of champagne. I had just signed my best ever contract, a five year deal, and was about to captain the side the following day against Arsenal and here he was offering me a drink, which I turned down. He asked me again and I couldn't tell if he was being serious or not, but because in football it was always the rule that you couldn't have a beer within 48 hours of a game I still said no, at which point he said "I won't ask you again" and virtually forced a beer into my hand.

Sacko, as usual, was in the background laughing at all of this and in the end we all ended up leaving Reidy's office in the Main Stand a little tipsy. Even for me and my drinking habits having just the one drink a day before a game was out of character, but it was nothing over board and in the end it did me no harm at all; not only was it my cross from the left wing that lead to the only goal of the game when Tony Adams put through his own net, but I ended up being given the Man of the Match award too!

That game was one of three in a row against Arsenal because we'd drawn at Highbury in the FA Cup the week before and had a replay four days after the league match. It turned out that Bally had broken his jaw in the match against Derby County and because he was in the stands for the first game we knew we could take the mick a bit and he would have to sit there and take it; we were always making fun of his bald patch and his big nose so Mickey Gray and I decided that if either of us scored we would do some sort of daft celebration. Sure enough, Mickey scored and all of the other lads joined in with us as we patted our heads and put a hand over our noses, but I think Bally saw the funny side of it.

After drawing the first game and then beating them in the league we fancied getting through in the replay but in the end Arsenal's class told and they won 2-0; who knows, maybe I should have had a drink before that game too! To be fair to us, we had one or two younger lads in the side that night due to injuries and it was another one where we conceded a wonder goal; Denis Bergkamp did a couple of step over's on the edge of the box before curling it past Lionel Perez and again, like the Eric Cantona effort it still gets shown on TV now.

There was nothing Lionel could have done with that shot, but it is fair to say that he could be quite erratic to play in front of at times. It would affect your own performance and that of the other lads at the back because you are second guessing everything and it complicates matters, but off the pitch I found him to be canny at

And here we are at the old farm house

One of my favourite pictures of me with Liam

9 March 1996. Up against familiar opponents in Derby County battling here with Dean Sturridge

130

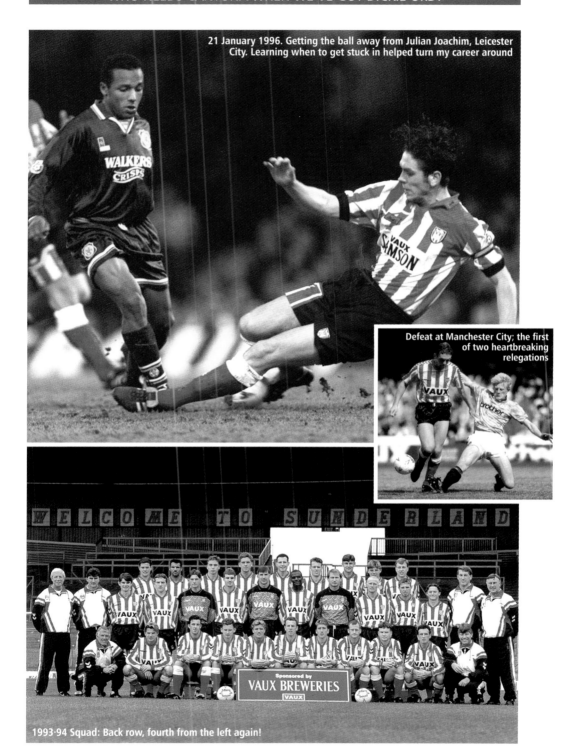

21 January 1996. Getting the ball away from Julian Joachim, Leicester City. Learning when to get stuck in helped turn my career around

Defeat at Manchester City; the first of two heartbreaking relegations

WELCOME TO SUNDERLAND

Sponsored by
VAUX BREWERIES
VAUX

1993-94 Squad: Back row, fourth from the left again!

The team spirit when we won Division One was excellent, and the celebrations were great

It was a season of personal success too

This is for Mam and Dad, seeing as they originally missed the goal

21 August 1996. Celebrating scoring the fourth goal of the night as we beat Forest 4-1

134

Golf in Marbella. Back, l to r: Chod (Crud's mate), Paul Dawson (Stewy's brother), Stewy, Crud, Me. Front: Richie Rodden, Peter McGurk (Stewy's bank manager), Dad

THE Richard Ord TESTIMONIAL

Sunderland AFC V Steaua Bucharest

Official Programme: £1.50

Wednesday July 29th 1998, Kick off 7.45pm

My testimonial season was amazing, but the game was a let down

Getting my marching orders for the second time in a month against Boro

The last rites; one of my final games as a professional

135

The twins strike a pose

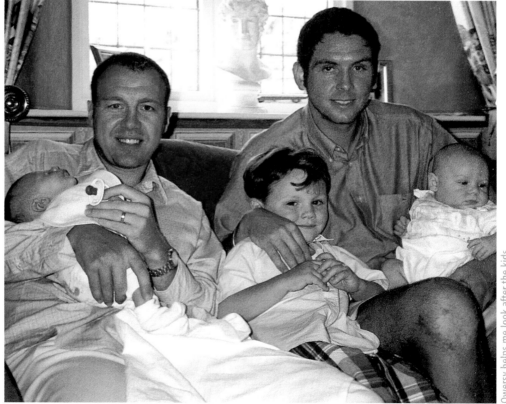

Owersy helps me look after the kids

first and felt that we got on. Obviously you look at an average Premier League squad today and there is perhaps one or two home grown lads making up the numbers alongside players from abroad, but back then it was the other way round and as we didn't have many foreign players in the squad at that time I tried to make an effort with him; he didn't look it or behave like it on the pitch, but he was a bit of a recluse so I think he appreciated the company. He did his weights every morning and I would go in and have a bit chat on with him and he was always saying to me "I love you, Dickie" in his French accent.

He was a nice bloke; he had a nice wife and a nice family but about half way through the season we went out as a squad for a Chinese meal at a restaurant on North Bridge Street called the Royal Garden close to where the Stadium of Light was being built and we fell out big style over something and nothing. Honestly, I was always making a fuss of him and trying to make him feel part of the group, so I chose to sit next to him but one of the other lads started taking the mick a bit and Lionel took it out on me instead. It was such a daft little thing that I can't even remember who it was or what exactly they said even, but it was one of the youth team players and what he was saying wasn't even anything out of the ordinary, it was just the general banter you get between blokes, but it hit a nerve with Lionel for some reason and we ended up having a bust up.

We had the place to ourselves and Bally had to calm it all down. I don't normally like getting into arguments but I felt worked up because he was having a pop at me even though I had nothing to do with it, never mind the fact I had made an effort to welcome him. I know that there were some that saw him as arrogant and he probably did love himself a bit too much but I had always seen past that side of things and it was a shame that we drifted because we were not used to there being rifts amongst the squad.

After the Arsenal cup game we went on a run of six games without a win and that meant we suddenly had to start looking at the clubs beneath us. Relegation never felt on the cards and it certainly wasn't something that was playing on our minds up until that point but with us starting to get sucked into the relegation scrap Bally called us all together to give us a bit of a rallying call. After a good start we were mid table and in good shape come Christmas but you see it so often in sport, once you lose a couple of games quickly the wheels come off and that was happening to us. We all knew where our problems were though, and given how few goals we had scored as a team we were doing well to be still be as high as we were.

The next game after our get together was at home to Manchester United so we put everything we had into it and won 2-1. That was one of the best games I ever had for Sunderland I would say, we had a few young lads in the team that day too and it made the senior players such as myself have to think that little bit more and to look out for them. I remember the game vividly even now and I suppose any player that beats Manchester United would because they were, and still are, that big a scalp.

It was only when Mel scored a freakish own goal late on that they came into things, and that was only because the sun was in his eyes and he had to take a bit of a blind swing at the ball. He took some stick for that one when he walked into the pub that night but the way we played in games like that showed that we were not a million miles off being the complete article. That season we beat four of the eventual top six at home but three of those were by a single goal so we were always under pressure to score first.

When I think back to some of the other games I realise that if we had put our early chances away we could have sat back just that little bit. It wasn't our game really to play defensively but if you have a lead to build on it is so much easier for you, and so much harder for the opposition. The first game against Manchester United was a good example; for the first twenty or so minutes we were well in the game, but we missed a couple of good chances and once United scored were on the back foot and when you are chasing the game teams of that level can suddenly turn it on and rip you apart.

After beating them at home however we were all keen to try and start building up a head of steam again. The following week though Chelsea tore us apart and it took the wind out of us totally, but it was a couple of home games after that which I feel did the most damage. Firstly there was the Nottingham Forest game where they equalised late on through Des Lyttle; he was a right back and wouldn't you know it, it was one of the only goals he scored in all of his life. It was a real blow to concede late on when we had looked good enough for the win, and then there was the night match against Southampton where it didn't matter how many chances or corners we had, we just couldn't score and ended up losing 1-0.

The week before we had gone ahead against Middlesbrough through Darren Williams and that proves my point about getting the first goal, because after that we were good enough to see the game out fairly easily. When we were dominating Southampton though but kept missing chances you could sense there would be a sucker punch and it had a major impact as they eventually finished the season just a point ahead of us. One good aspect though had been the arrival of Chris Waddle, who had made his debut in that match against Forest and despite only being at the club for a short space of time provided the spark that nearly kept us in the league.

Back when we were celebrating winning the Division Three title Gordon Armstrong had told me that he thought I would play for England. I thought for a long time that the two sending offs I'd had earlier in the season had put pay to any suggestion of it becoming reality, but it wasn't quite as far as it went and the arrival of Waddler perhaps put me in the England manager Glen Hoddle's thoughts again. The pair were close mates and of course will always be remembered for their duet single Diamond Lights, so Waddler would be on the phone to him during trips to away games saying things like 'I've got Dickie here, do you want a word with him?' and trying to pass me over.

With him having spent a couple of seasons in France and then in the Premier League with Sheffield Wednesday whilst we were drifting in Division One Waddler hadn't really seen me at close quarters before arriving at the club, but we used to mess about after training trying to hit the cross bar from the half way line and all of that and he was impressed with some of my skills. Even though he was only at he club for a short while we got quite close and spent a few nights out together; he was a nice lad, and quite down to earth really given how big a name he was and he pushed my cause a lot.

I would shy away and tell him to leave it whenever he brought England up though, but I also found that Hoddle's assistant John Gorman had watched me a lot that season so I must have been fairly close to a call up at one point. The problem is though that you never hear the full story so I don't know what cost me in the end; Hoddle knew about me, but it never happened and obviously that was a shame, although the way I try to look at it is that at least I was there or there abouts.

Had I been called up that of course would have been an amazing experience, not least because, as I have mentioned before, I loved Glenn as a player when I was growing up. I used to model myself a bit on him because obviously I was quite tall and played in centre midfield too, so would try and ping the ball about a bit like him. He was an unbelievable player, I remember that he played at Roker Park one time and as I watched him I was in awe. His replacement as England manager, Kevin Keegan, was another player I loved watching as a kid. I used to love his enthusiasm and his commitment so he was another one I tried to play like; although I didn't model myself on him as much because of that hair! I've met them both since watching them as a lad and Kevin in particular was one of the nicest blokes I have ever met to be honest; meeting one of your heroes from when you were a kid can be quite daunting obviously but he put me at ease.

Waddler's finest moment came the day we played Everton in the last league game at Roker Park. Regardless of any relegation concerns it was always going to be emotional but with the situation being as it was we had to put that all to one side and concentrate on the game. Waddler scored a memorable free kick in front of the Fulwell End, it was excellent. He used to practise those with me when we were staying back after training and he said to me when we got the free kick "I'm going to score here Dickie" and I think I just rolled me eyes and said "aye, reetio mate", but sure enough he put it away beautifully and in the end we won 3-0.

After the game the players did a lap of the pitch to applaud the fans because it was the last home match of the season. I threw my shirt to a good mate of mine Stevie Collins and when I saw him the in bar afterwards I asked him if he got it and he said "no, I gave it to the little lad stood next to me"; I was gutted, if he didn't want it I would have liked to have kept it for myself!

I have to admit that at that point I thought that was it, I thought we were safe. We didn't know what was about to come round the corner though, and that stands both for the team and for me, because that game was where I first started experiencing the back pain that would have a hand in me eventually leaving Sunderland. I remember going down during the game and getting a twinge along my hamstring. It went all the way to my foot and I had no idea what it was; I didn't get cramp during this point of my career but that was what it felt like; Duncan Ferguson was playing and he was always good for a bit of a craic on during the game so he was telling me to stop being soft and to get up, but the physio had to come on and treat me and whilst the pain initially went it later proved to be the beginning of the end.

This was all to blow up down the line however and after the match all we wanted was to celebrate the moment. That was a big weekend sporting wise for the city because as well as the last league game at Roker Park, Billy Hardy was fighting for the WBO and IBF World Featherweight boxing titles against Naseem Hamed and so I had organised a big coach to take us down. The trip there was great because everybody was buzzing due to the Everton result; Lee Howie was part of the trip and because he had brought two or three bottles of whisky he was just up and down the bus all the time plying us with drink and we were all mortal by the time we arrived.

Come the fight and Lee was trying to start up all the chanting but Billy got a couple of bangs in the early stages and that was it, the fight was over and we where all a bit shell shocked for him. We were all meant to be staying in the same hotel as Billy so we went back there to wait for him to come in and when he arrived he was totally silent; he came in and walked straight to me to give me a cuddle; he knew I'd organised the trip and the first thing he said to any of us was "sorry Dickie".

The lads were having none of it though, and we all told him how proud of him we were. His nose was all over his face however, so I asked if that was from the punch that knocked him out and he just said "no, that was his first jab". It was only then that we realised how unreal a boxer Naseem was, but that was it from Billy for the night; the rest of his family stayed downstairs for a drink but he couldn't face it.

Billy always was a big Sunderland fan and he was close mates with Benno. Before one game we were all having rubs before kick off and Billy walked in; he'd only had his ears pinned and all of the lads jumped all over it "you look different class son, how have you managed that" and he was telling us all "I've spent all my money, that's how" and to be fair to him he took all the gags. He would come down to training or to use the treatment room too and there were times when we would do a lot of stuff together if ever I was coming back from one of my injuries. He was as fit as a lop but a boxer needs different stamina levels, so whilst he could do all of the jumps and stretches if we had to do something like a twelve minute run he had no chance. When we would have to do laps round the ash track at Roker Park the players could do nine or ten whereas Billy could maybe manage six, but in other drills he would blow you away.

Our final game of the season was away at Wimbledon and we started the day out of the relegation zone. Our destiny was in our own hands, and as was the case when we played Manchester City in 1991, there were thousands of Sunderland fans in the stands. Yet again, we felt that if we scored first we would have settled down and gone on to win but Paul Stewart missed a great chance when he was through on goal and after that we fell apart and ended up losing the game 1-0. After feeling comfortable in the Premier League for so long we had got ourselves into a position where we could go down and so were very nervous, but Wimbledon had nothing to play for and you could see they were playing with a bit of freedom.

We huffed and puffed but got nowhere and I felt as if the world had ended when the final whistle went. Coventry City had started the day below us in the table but were winning their game at Tottenham Hotspur, but because the kick off to that match had been delayed we had a lifeline and all piled into the changing rooms to get to a radio. If Spurs scored in those last few minutes we would have stayed up and it seemed as if they were creating chance after chance, so it was like torture in there as we all listened in. Everybody was willing Spurs on but I could just tell from the way things were going that it wasn't going to happen and all I could think about was my family. You are talking about people's lives when you think about relegation, and I knew how nervous my wife and parents were before the game.

They felt for me and it really got to them. When it was finally confirmed that Coventry had won and we would be going down by a single point I rang Sonia and she was distraught, and it took me so much longer than before to get over it too. I wasn't just a bit part player any more and to be relegated by such a slim margin made it so much harder to take than in 1991. Actually being a Sunderland fan didn't help either, all my mates pulled round me and everybody was ringing me trying to pick me up in the weeks afterwards but I felt for them just as much as for myself and there was no way of me being able to bury my head in the sand.

Even now I sometimes stop to think 'what if', because had we managed to avoid relegation we could have built up something good. The squad that we had was ready in so many ways, but it was another case of so near yet so far and just to make it even worse, the whole thing was filmed by the BBC for a documentary called Premier Passions. They got a lot of access to things behind the scenes and it was quite ground breaking to be able to get that close to such a high profile club, but I hated it personally because every time they were in filming we seemed to get beat.

If anybody were to watch the programmes back they'll see that I never did an interview with the producers because I saw it as a distraction. They were there mostly on match days when you had other things to concentrate on, although some of the other lads loved the extra attention; I reckon they thought we were film stars! Seeing the programme when it was broadcast the following season just brought everything back up again too, but what most people viewing from the outside took from it was the way Reidy would go on at us sometimes, as I think the language shocked a lot of watchers.

One of the games that was featured was the trip to Aston Villa and on that occasion it was Sacko that came in and started having a go at us at half time. You could see on camera that most of us were sat in the changing rooms with our heads down and it wasn't because we weren't paying attention, but getting a rollicking is embarrassing enough without the cameras there. That game was another one where we didn't do too badly and you couldn't pick a winner for the majority of the match, but they had that one moment where they were able to finish us off and that was it.

Sacko was right to have a go at us as the game had been there for the taking, and when you look at the amount of times we where in a match for long periods but came away without any points you realise why they were always trying to raise us just that little bit more. If something needed saying, neither Reidy or Sacko would have any problems saying it, and as they were usually right you had to take it in so whereas some of the team talks shocked viewers we had accepted them long before. They knew football inside out so there was never a time where one of them would have a go and it wasn't warranted and I can't remember anybody ever having a go back at them because we all knew that what was being said made sense.

Things with Paul Bracewell were not quite as straight forward for me however, stemming from his last period at the club when we never really saw eye to eye. As assistant manager now, he took pre match warm ups amongst other things but the main stuff was always done by either Sacko or Reidy himself so it wasn't a massive problem; it just always felt as if there was an atmosphere between us.

Don't get me wrong, he could be alright most of the time and I tried to get on with things, because a changing room needs to be as open as possible and at our place team spirit had been such a big part of us getting promoted. Purely as a player he was great, but I sometimes felt he could be a bit stand offish and he was one of the few people within football that I didn't get on with well. He was totally unlike Reidy, and yet the pair were good friends.

At least our relegation had not been actually confirmed at Roker Park and after the Wimbledon game we had a friendly against Liverpool to mark the closing of the old place. Most of the players were interested by the move and looking forward to it, but I don't think they were bothered by it in the same way myself or the fans were and it wasn't the same thing for people that didn't grow up with the club. I was devastated by moving, I honestly felt there was nowhere like it; even the smell of the place gave me goose bumps. I had a lot of memories tied up with Roker Park both as a fan and a player and it was part of my childhood and my family.

The Liverpool game was to be the last ever football match played at Roker Park and Reidy made me captain for the evening. It was a sentimental gesture more than

143

anything else and another nice touch from him, but with us having just been relegated as well as wanting to say goodbye it was an emotional night. I went close with a half volley in front of the Fulwell End but it was John Mullin that would score the last goal there, and it was a good one; he turned well to finish and the match ended 1-0.

There were a lot of thoughts going through my mind that night but the thing I remember most was trying to unscrew the sign from the away team dressing room door, but because I was pushing too hard it swung open and all of the Liverpool lads who were inside started laughing at me. It had been my job to keep that part of the ground clean and tidy when I was on my YTS all those years before so I thought it would be a good thing to keep, and I still have it now along with the one from the home team room as well.

It was now time for a new era and the move to the Stadium of Light ready for the next season. Relegation meant we would be starting in Division One, but from a purely personal point of view I was only looking forward. There were a couple more of the supporters' branches Player of the Season awards for me and I had finished third in the Echo Star Ratings for the season so it was a far cry from when I was struggling to even get a look in. Over the last three seasons I had established myself as being one of the first names on the team sheet; but whereas the Stadium of Light was supposed to be a bright new start for everybody, for me the following season signalled the beginning of the end.

The opening of the stadium was the start of a new era for the club, but not for me

CHAPTER FOURTEEN

In the dark

The Stadium of Light opened with a game against Ajax, and having played in the last match at Roker Park I am proud to have played in this game too; it is a nice thing to be able to say both for myself and for my family.

A lot of clubs had been forced to move ground but this was one of the biggest new stadiums in the country so Sunderland rightly wanted to make a big thing of it. Work was being carried out right until the day of the game and there was all sorts of pre match entertainment lined up, but the match itself was quite big because we had just come down from the Premiership and this was a test against a top side.

It finished 0-0 but the fact we played so well and had this new stadium to play in meant that once again, we were expecting to be one of the promotion favourites. I'd be lying if I said I was a fan of the Stadium of Light though, football had moved on and the club needed a new ground but for me you will never be able to recreate the atmosphere at Roker Park. I'm old fashioned in the sense that I prefer the older more traditional grounds and feel they are more intimidating to the opposition, although I do accept that sadly there was not the room to improve at Roker and that the club could not become as big as it has now had the move not taken place.

We beat Manchester City in the first league game at the ground and I played in that game too. The initial wow factor of the Stadium of Light meant we were playing in front of some decent crowds, often much bigger than Roker Park could have managed, but our form, particularly on the road was hitty missy as we started trying to get used to playing in Division One. The game down at Reading where we lost 4-0 was a particular low point and after that Mel dropped out for Jody Craddock, who had arrived at the club the day before we played against Ajax.

I only managed another two games after that myself as my back problems started to really take hold. By this point I was struggling through the pain barrier just to get the games finished and it was obvious something wasn't right; and I knew I had to be honest and talk to Reidy about it. We beat Oxford United 3-1 and I should have got on the score sheet because I had two good chances, but I missed one of them completely and hit the bar with the other. I would have liked to be able to say that I had scored at the Stadium of Light but after the game I had to approach the gaffer and even though I had tried to keep it to myself before then I think he already knew it himself that something was up.

Reidy arranged for me to see a specialist through in Newcastle and I was told that I had prolapsed discs. As they were too close to my spinal nerves though, having them operated on was not going to be possible and the only option I had if I wanted to carry on would be to take injections to numb the pain instead. It was no surprise to find I had something serious because it had almost become too much to bare; my Dad has had a lot of back issues so it was probably hereditary and with all of my growing problems when I was younger this was bound to happen.

In the meantime I had been rested during the League Cup but had kept trying to battle on through our league games. I then had to go through to the Nuffield and have an epidural, which is usually given to ladies when they are giving birth to try and help with the labour. My doctor put the needle into my spine though and it was horrendous, he was looking for the spot and kept having to try again and again and I was in agony throughout the procedure. It was the same thing when I went through the next time too so the doctor decided that he couldn't give me anymore injections, and from this point I knew it was going to be an issue for the rest of my career and would be something that I would have to learn to manage.

I didn't ever let myself think it was going to stop me playing football though and I wanted to be back in the first team as quickly as possible once I had allowed it to rest. Since dropping out of the team though after we drew against Swindon Town the side had gone another fifteen games without defeat and Darren Williams and Jody Craddock had started clicking well together in the middle of defence.

The team was on fire again and were chasing down the two automatic promotion spots, and at the heart of it all were Quinny and a certain striker called Kevin Phillips, who Reidy had brought in during the summer after he had allowed Paul Stewart to go. Stewy actually scored against us that season when playing for Stoke City when I first dropped out of the side but I think he would always admit that the real highlight of his career was when he later came back up to the area and did a favour for my mate Pratty and turned out for the Demi!

Kev had clicked with Quinny though and nobody could live with them. The club was starting to get under Quinny's skin and he was becoming a firm favourite with the fans; he was like the pied piper whereever he went and I'll never forget the time me and Mickey Gray went with him for a 'quiet drink' in Bournemouth. We'd just played in London and Reidy wanted us to stay down south for a bit of time off and then some training in the better weather, and on the bus in we saw an O'Neills and decided we would go in the following day. We arrived at 11 o'clock in the morning and there wasn't a soul in, but the landlord was on the phone the second he saw Quinny and within half an hour the queue was out of the door. Quinny was posing for photos with people's babies and all of this whilst me and Mickey were just sat in the corner gobsmacked.

We soon moved on from the Guinness to Irish whiskey, and as the day went on Mickey ended up doing all the Irish dancing with the locals before getting carried back to our hotel at 7 o'clock in the evening because he was well gone. I could barely stand either but lasted till about 9 o'clock before getting taken back to the hotel by Gordon Ellis and yet here Quinny was, still drinking and still chatting on to all of these people like nothing you had seen; I don't know how he managed it. Me and Mickey were blotto and yet he was able to keep going for hours before walking himself back without any bother, only to find me out cold on my bed, stark naked and with the remains of a KFC bucket of chicken all over the room! I'd never had one before so after seeing one on the way back insisted that Gordon took me back out; when Quinny got back to the room he saw all these bones on the floor and thought I'd murdered somebody.

Mickey of course was another big part of the team at left back by now and I will have to remind him one day that he only got his chance in the first place because of all my injury problems! Mickey is another great lad, but he always got called 'two pint Mick'; not though because he drank twice as quickly as the rest of us but because that's all he needed and he would be drunk. After he left Sunderland and went to Blackburn Rovers he was back up home once and was drinking in Seaham so I got a call from Aidy saying I should pop down, but when I got there and saw him it turned out he had changed his accent. I gave him some right stick about it and all of a sudden he was talking like a Mackem again; I know he does a lot of commentary now on the radio but I keep missing him so I've got no idea what he sounds like these days!

Now we had a new ground, a decent team and were playing some entertaining football. The side were much more attacking than the one I had played in when we got promoted two seasons earlier and the place was buzzing, so I was desperate to be a part of it. I would play the odd game for the reserves and then have to rest my back, but I would always be able to play well and as the injury problems were not holding me back during the matches themselves anymore I was just waiting for a chance to return to the first team.

In all I was an unused substitute 13 times that season but after seeing our unbeaten run go against Tranmere Rovers in the FA Cup before losing again against Norwich City in the next game I was brought on from the bench at the end of January 1998 to replace Darren Williams against Port Vale.

With Darren injured I kept my place and was really pleased with my performance away at Wolverhampton Wanderers the following week. It was a really close game and we only won it right at the end when Bally scored, but my return was only to be temporary as Chris Makin was soon back and I had to make way. Chris had been another of the new arrivals over the summer and had made an impressive start to his time at the club at right back, so when he was fit again I could hardly complain that Reidy wanted to shuffle things around to accommodate him, with Darren Holloway coming into the centre for me.

Darren had come through the ranks like me and was young and full of energy, he too was a versatile player, and it all meant that my last ever home game for

Sunderland was on 17 February 1998. With the team having scored four during my return against Port Vale we did it again to extract a bit of revenge against Reading for the defeat at Elm Park earlier in the season and whilst I didn't know it then, looking back now I can accept that winning comfortably in front of almost 40,000 fans was as good a way as any to bow out.

Our next game was away at Middlesbrough and although we lost, the side went back on another massive unbeaten run afterwards and it meant my involvement was kept to a minimum; in fact probably the closest I got to putting on the shirt again for a long while was when I was asked to model one of the possible away kits for the following season! Some of the designs were horrendous, but the idea was that fans got to choose which one would be used and I suppose it is quite ironic that the one that eventually got the nod was being modelled by Jody, who along with Darren had been getting picked ahead of me in the side.

After losing to Tranmere in the FA Cup we were back down there in April for the league fixture, which was played on a Friday night due to the Grand National being scheduled for the following day. This prompted Aidy to arrange a big weekend for all of the Murton and Seaham lads but because there had been an accident on the motorway they didn't get to Prenton Park until after the gates had been closed. For some reason the stewards decided to allow them in through the main stand and guided them along the touch line towards the away end, but I had been named as a sub so of course didn't know any of this until suddenly they started streaming past the Sunderland bench half way through the game; Sacko was saying hello to them all and laughing away but Reidy was going berserk, and it was me that got the blame!

Sunderland won the game 2-0 but I didn't get brought on, and afterwards we all had a night out in Liverpool. I could understand the reasons for me not being in the side, but it hadn't got any easier to take and with Mel also out of the picture the pair of us ended up drinking all night and didn't go to bed. We were sat in the breakfast area of our hotel the following morning drinking bottles of champagne and as the rest of the squad made their way down we told them that if they wanted to sit with us they would have to order one too. In the end the hotel ran out of champagne and we all jumped onto a bus to go to watch the Grand National absolutely plastered.

I don't know what we were playing at to be honest because it couldn't have done our chances of getting back into the team any good, but Mel and I didn't go to bed that night ether; we'd stayed up for 48 hours and had been drinking non stop and come the Monday had to report at the stadium for a reserve game down at Leicester City. TC was running the side and when he saw the state of us he just ordered us both to get some coffee down our necks and then try and get some kip on the journey down; it probably wasn't the best example to set to the younger players either but I was perhaps in self destruct mode because things had gone so wrong for me and I had once again found that my body was letting me down.

Despite finishing twelve points behind us the year we won Division One, Leicester had come up with us via the play offs and finished ninth in the Premiership whilst we got relegated. They were having another decent season this time around too and it drove home to me and Mel that had we been able to build more on that championship winning team things could have been a lot different for Sunderland, there was no obvious difference between the two reserve sides either and it was like the good old days for me and Mel at the back; we were unbelievable given the state we were in and the game finished 2-2, which meant we had won the Pontins League Division One title.

Sunderland always had a strong reserve team during this era and since moving to the Stadium of Light home games were played at Durham City's New Ferens Park, which would be a ground I would become very familiar with once my career in the professional game was over. The move to the Stadium had brought with it a lot of changes to the club, and with the sport in general becoming more forward thinking Reidy and the club staff were paying more and more attention to the little details and more modern ideas such as sports science. We were still training at the Charlie Hurley Centre then, and whilst it had nothing on the current Academy of Light in terms of other facilities the surface there was always fantastic. Before Reidy came we would still have to get changed at Roker Park though and then drive through to Cleadon or Whitburn but he changed that and insisted on Portakabin's being installed at the Charlie Hurley Centre so that we could get ready on site.

It was a good move because it made Roker Park and then the Stadium of Light special, as now we would only be there if it was match day. Before this all there had been at the training ground was a little club house type of affair with a small tea bar, but that got turned into Reidy's head tennis court because he was always playing that after training. The Portakabin's were set up and there was one for the youth players, one for the senior players and a third one, which had a dinning room in. That was the first time that we started sitting down together to eat after training;

before that you were just left to you own devices, but now you could have your breakfast there and some lunch and whilst nobody was made to stay it was good for team spirit because everybody was having a craic on, and I suppose it was a way of the club keeping tabs on your diet.

Drinking was still at large in football in the main at this point, certainly with the majority of British players anyway, but you could see at the top clubs that attitudes were shifting a bit and more importance was being put on what you eat too as people woke up to the benefits of a healthy diet. I had got into a routine when things were going well under Reidy though where I was going to a chippy in Fence Houses every Friday night before a home game and daft as it sounds, it actually seemed to help my performances.

It wasn't the done thing to be having fish and chips the night before a game but I got into this habit somehow, it was a ritual really and another one of those superstitions. Come the morning of the game though I wouldn't be able to eat much at all, and that was actually the case throughout my career. I might have had a drink of tea but I could have very little food wise because I wouldn't be able to keep it down and it was only after the game had finished that I would be able to force myself to eat something proper. If we went away and stayed over night we would meet at half eleven for a pre match meal and I might have managed a tiny bit of toast with a slice of banana but that would be about it, again it probably isn't what the nutritionists would recommend but I would have made sure that I had fed myself up in the days leading before the game so I could cope.

The final two games of the regular season were both away from home and I was brought back onto the bench as cover. Towards the end of March we had squeezed into second place and that would have been good enough for automatic promotion, but we lost the first of those two games away at Ipswich Town and it meant that we had followed up being relegated from the Premiership with a record high tally by then earning the highest total of points not to have gained automatic promotion from Division One, and it meant we would have to settle with a place in the Play Offs instead.

The first leg of our semi final against Sheffield United was away at Bramall Lane and we knew that we were that strong at home all we needed to do was stay in touch. Bally scored a beauty for us in the first half to put us in the driving seat and from that point we were confident that even if we lost the game we would be in with a shout of going through the tie on aggregate. I've seen Bally stand up and pull us

151

through situations time and time again, but he was a player as well and I think sometimes people didn't realise it, they just assumed he was a work horse or a clogger and nothing more. His partnership with Lee Clark that season was another major part of the side's success too, but the Clarky situation was another where my initial friendliness ended up biting me on the backside.

Lots of players have come from Tyneside and done well enough at Sunderland that their background wasn't an issue, but we knew when he signed that it might be different for Lee because he had actually played for Newcastle United too and had always made it clear that he had been a fan of the club from being a young boy. I would ring Lee up then and invite him through on a Sunday for a couple of drinks to try and make him feel welcome; we got on like a house on fire but he let himself down a bit a year or so after I had moved and the way he left the club was a shame. He was a lovely lad at heart and he has since said it himself that he let himself down, but he was a good player too and it cost both parties when he had to move on.

That season though he was an ever present in the league and was immense. He worked so well with Bally because they dovetailed and although we ended up losing that first leg to Sheffield United the spade work had been done ready for the return game at the Stadium of Light, which turned out to be one of the ground's first classics. A lot of people felt that was the night when the old Roker Roar finally moved over to the stadium, but from my point of view it was actually the Bramall Lane match that was to prove most significant.

When I came on as a substitute for Chris Makin on 10th May 1998 it was not only my last appearance for Sunderland but also my last game as a professional footballer. I was an unused substitute again for the home tie and was then named as part of the travelling squad for the Play Off Final against Charlton Athletic but on the day of the game Reidy had to tell me that Chris was fit again so I wasn't even going to be named as a substitute.

I'd played at Wembley so early in my career of course but then missed out on three much more important games and the news absolutely floored me. I was as desperate as ever to be part of things and to do my bit and whilst for the 1990 Play Offs and the 1992 FA Cup Final I'd at least known in advance that I wasn't going to feature the fact that I had been part of the initial squad and taken part in training meant it was even more distressing. It was all I could do to shake all of the lads' hands before the match and to then have to watch on, helpless, tore me apart.

The game has since become one of the most famous matches at Wembley but anybody that saw it knows how draining it was for the players to have been so close to winning before losing the penalty shoot out and no amount of praise for being involved in such an exciting game will make up for missing out on promotion in such a cruel way. Even though I was hurting so much inside, both for myself and for the club, I was then one of the ones trying to put a brave face on things and lift the lads on the way back up afterwards but how much of that was me trying to ignore my own situation I don't know.

We ended up stopping the coach at some random pub and having a lock in. As a group we got wasted and that was what we needed at that point in time, Bally and Quinny were rallying the troops and making sure people were going to take the experience into the following season and turn it into a good thing; and I got up and did my Ru Char Char number to try and help pick everybody up. It's my signature tune if you will; it is just a daft chant really and it ends with everybody jumping about 'singing in the rain'. It's a Murton thing I think, my mate Stevie Collins was doing it in the Murton Inn one night and it stuck with me, so I belt it out at times and it raises a few smiles.

It was to be another miserable summer for us all though, and one in which I did a lot of thinking. Relegation from the Premiership the year prior was awful, but this season had started with my own situation being pretty clear. I had become the valued member of the team that I had wanted to be for so long, but in the end the 1997-98 season turned out to be like so many before it; with me on the fringes.

Take a good look, because there wasn't to be many more shots of me in action

CHAPTER FIFTEEN

Doctors ORDers

I returned to pre season for 1998-99 with my head in a mess. I had rested my back but deep down I was expecting it to be an issue somewhere along the line, and when the gaffer brought Paul Butler in from Bury I started seeing problems that weren't even there and decided that he must have wanted rid of me. Then, Ray Harford, who had been my coach way back when I was with England Under 21s, was now in charge of Queens Park Rangers and having seen that I had been out of the side for most of the previous season made an approach just at the time I was having all of these doubts.

I don't think Reidy ever wanted me to go, but he probably felt I had a right to know there was some interest in me and when he spoke to me about it I just jumped to even more conclusions. I tried reading between the lines and took him telling me about it as him saying he wanted me out and so I threw the toys out of the pram big style. We were down in Devon for a pre season tour but I left that to go over to talk to Ray and because he was telling me he wanted me to be captain and all of this I made a snap decision and agreed to moving.

At this point I still had nearly four years left on my contract at Sunderland and here QPR were offering me less money, but it was never about the cash in truth. I was in a mood about not being in the team and wasn't thinking straight; I'd taken the hump and spat the dummy out plain and simple, and that's all it ever was. I didn't want to leave Sunderland one bit, and I had worked my way back into the set up before so should have hung around and tried to do the same again; I just wish I could have seen it like that at the time.

Reidy even said in the newspapers at the time that he didn't want me to leave, but there were a couple of contractual issues at the Sunderland end that I wasn't happy with so when he rang me and said he wanted me to play in a pre season friendly before I signed anything I did it again; I took a huff because of the way I now felt the club were treating me and I told him to forget it.

Sacko 's bottom lip started going when I told him I was leaving and he said to me "please don't go Dickie", but I had backed myself into a corner and thought everybody was against me. I regret it now though of course, definitely, and it is probably the biggest regret of my life - and yet it was all over something and nothing. Sunderland was my club, and despite that on 23 July 1998 I signed for QPR when I should have been knuckling down ready for what was about to be a brilliant season.

Whilst Sunderland went on to win the title by a distance my time at QPR was a nightmare literally from day one. I went there all fired up and ready for something new, but I got injured in my first training session and it was all finished before I had even played a game for them. We were having a small sided kick about and when I went to block the ball as someone took a shot the force jarred my knee and I did everything; cruciate ligament, nerves, the lot, and I would never be able to manage a recovery.

Some onlookers will have seen the fact that I'd dropped out of the Sunderland side with a back injury and then gone down to QPR but not actually played for them and assumed it was a fiddle or that Sunderland had done the dirty on QPR. I knew that those were the type of whispers that were doing the rounds at the time but I can honestly say that was never the case, Reidy didn't even mention my back to me during that pre season and I was never worried about passing a medical because whilst my problems were there and would need to be managed they weren't stopping me getting through the games.

The rumour that it was some sort of con was just that, although I can see how some people could put two and two together and come up with something completely different given the circumstances. The truth is a lot more boring though, these new injuries were unconnected to anything that had gone on before and it was simply a case of it being one of those things nobody could have predicted; that type of block tackle was something I would have done hundreds of times in my career but typical of my luck something so routine ended up being the thing that ended my career.

We moved down to a club house in Watford but we'd kept our home back in Hetton le Hill and when Sonia found out she was pregnant again her and Liam went back north. I remember one morning going to QPR's training ground in a taxi and getting a call from her, she was screaming down the phone "I can't believe it, we are having twins" and I just started rolling about laughing; the taxi driver thought I was an idiot. I was going to be out of the house all day though and Liam was still young so when the lease was up on the house it made sense for her to be closer to family and I would just stay down in London during the week, get some treatment, and travel back on the Friday afternoon.

Luckily, I had a mate that worked on the railways so I got to go via first class for free and obviously homesickness wasn't the issue it would have been when I was younger, but the whole situation was far from easy for any us and being on my own for large parts of the time when I was coming to terms with an injury and missing my family made it all the harder for me.

QPR were in the same division as Sunderland but didn't start the season well at all, and who were their first opponents of the campaign? Sunderland of course, at the Stadium of Light. My injury meant I missed out on what would have been a surreal debut, and by September Ray was sacked. The club had brought some players in on top contracts in the years before my arrival and were paying fortunes in wages to some of them, but it was more than they could afford really and they were in big trouble both on and off the pitch for a lot of the time I was contracted to them.

I had a fair bit of interaction with the other lads in the squad, even though I was unable to play. Gavin Peacock, Mike Sheron and Danny Maddix were all there and they were fantastic with me considering I didn't know them from Adam, they honestly were. I used to go out with Kevin Gallon a lot too because he was injured at the same time and he was a great lad, he would let me come and stay with him if I was down for a few days and so we became quite close.

The club as a whole was very homely in fact, and it was similar to how Sunderland used to be in some ways because it had a traditional old stadium and a lot of good people behind the scenes. I didn't have a problem with QPR at all, I just wished that I hadn't left Sunderland because then I might not have got into this mess with my knee. You look at Mel that season for example; he had been phased out the season before too but got back into the side and was a regular again for the rest of the season, and I couldn't help but think things might have improved for me too had I hung around and not been so rash. We won the Division One title that year with a record breaking 105 points and it was another one of those 'what might have been' situations.

Even though I was at QPR now Sunderland was still in my heart. I was always on the phone to the lads and if I could get along I would go to games just as a regular fan sitting in with the crowd. The following season for example I was in the away end when we beat Newcastle United in the pouring rain; me, Aidy and our pal Nutty Norman went and we got absolutely soaked. The Newcastle fans had spotted me at half time though and where hurling abuse at me, but because Aidy was wearing this big leather jacket he eyed up the biggest, mouthiest one of the lot and started reaching for an imaginary gun in his coat pocket and they all suddenly sat down and shut up! It shows you how stupid this group were to have fallen for something so daft, but afterwards as we came out some kid ran up and punched Norman right in the face; the lad got arrested straight away but Norman couldn't understand why it was him that got hit and not me!

Obviously that wasn't something I would have been able to do however had I still been playing and I sometimes wonder how I would have felt had I actually got more involved at QPR, because I had grown up with Sunderland and it was second nature, so to have gone on and done things elsewhere might have been different and at some point loyalties might have been split.

When Sunderland came to Loftus Road on the way to winning the league in January, Aidy put together another of his famous tours and filled the bus with all of the usual reprobates that I knew from home and through Aidy and Quinny had got to know the rest of the squad too. Kevin Phillips came back from a long term injury in the game and scored a beauty with the outside of his boot and Quinny snatched a goal right at the death to save Sunderland a point even though Bally had been wrongly sent off. The side were top of the league and already looking a good bet for promotion so all of the lads were well up for a night out in London.

When Aidy and the boys went to pick the players up at Swiss Cottage then, they were all suited and booted and ready to go. Sacko hadn't realised that this was the plan though and started going mad at me for not telling him about it and all of this, even though it was Aidy that was in charge; so not for the first time I was in bother because of Aidy! We told Sacko to just get on but because he didn't know there was an overnighter on the cards he hadn't packed anything and ended up having to borrow some gear from us, so there he was in this exclusive club Aidy had managed to blag us into, wearing a shirt and tie, some tracksuit bottoms and a pair of Quinny's shoes!

I was coming back up for a few days so travelled home with the rest of the group the next day. Aidy had arranged a stop off at some pub between Leeds and Wetherby where he had put on some entertainment and a buffet lunch and we had enough money left from the kitty to put some behind for a free bar so everybody was lapping it up. There were a couple of dancers up on stage and things got a bit wild to be honest, I stayed right out of it but there was always fun and games when lads like Nutty Norman, Pricey and Wadge were around to whip everybody up and we realised there was a bloke in filming us all on camera.

He had come with this comedian Aidy had booked and claimed to have just been filming his act, but a few of lads were put out by it because they were trying to unwind and they knew that in the wrong hands the tape could be taken out of context. At one point this video camera was going to be flushed down the toilet until the bloke agreed to wipe the footage and it was just as well; some of the daft stuff Nutty Norman and that lot got up to could never go to print, never mind be seen on tape!

When Sunderland confirmed promotion at the end of my first season away from the club I was watching it on TV in London on my own, upset with everything and feeling sorry for myself. The game was at Gigg Lane against Bury and when they were on the bus on their way back home I rang Bally to pass on my congratulations. Sacko got on the line too and you could hear all of the others hooting and hollering in the background so I had a little tear to myself afterwards because I knew that I shouldn't have been anywhere else but on that bus with them. Obviously I was really pleased for them all, both as a fan and a former teammate but I couldn't help feeling that I should have been there celebrating too.

Sunderland were the best side in that division by a country mile and deserved it, not least because they had just gone through two traumatic seasons and had overcome it as a group, but for me to be looking on from the outside when I had been a part of the club's ups and downs for so long was a real blow and did nothing for my frame of mind when I was trying to come back from the knee problems.

QPR had been sending me to see a specialist and in the end I had to have six different operations. I got my cruciate ligament done and two weeks later I was lying in the bath back up in the north east when I went to feel the bandage and could see something coming out of it. I shouted for Sonia to come up because I was panicking, so she took a closer look and said the bolt was actually sticking out through my skin.

I got on the phone to my doctor straight away and he was trying to tell me not to worry, but that is easy to say when you don't have a lump of metal sticking out of you! I was meant to be resting to allow my body time to heal, but instead I had to get the soonest train possible so I could see him face to face and spent the whole journey trying to work out what was going to happen. When I got there though he took a quick look at me, told me to stay put and then disappeared for a bit, and when he returned to the room he had this twelve inch screwdriver and took the bolt out there and then without anaesthetic or any sort of preparation, like he was working on a car engine or something.

The original procedure was quite innovative, but for whatever reason my operation didn't go to plan and it took a while to get my head around it all. It was all very surreal, but there wasn't much I could do about it really. You have to accept the medical advice you are given and there will always be an element of risk with these procedures, and by this point I believe QPR were looking into the possibility of getting their investment in me back through their insurance instead anyway.

The club were always supportive of me though, they were brilliant with me on a one to one level. With me getting injured in my first training session they could have taken a different attitude with me, but they tried to do right by me and the insurance was dealt with up the chain; it was not something I got involved with any more than was necessary.

Players do not always get involved in that type of thing; you were just expected to concentrate on playing. It is like the fees that sometimes got paid for players, for example I am not even sure how much QPR paid to Sunderland for me. The figure that got bandied about in the press was three quarters of a million but I don't know how true that was, clubs don't always release the full facts to the media for one or reason or another and I didn't feel the need to ask anyway.

After the work on my knee I had another big operation on the nerves down my back that attached to the perennial nerve in my leg; all of the problems with my knee were interconnected and I don't ever think the doctors fully knew what the best way to go about things was. I was awake for that and could feel my big toe twitch when the surgeon fiddled with my nerve endings, but after every procedure I would try and start training again and my knee would always end up going from underneath me.

No matter what I tried I just didn't feel right at all. QPR couldn't have done enough for me and were willing to keep trying to look for an answer but come half way through the second season I'd had enough. I was stopping at a house in the centre of London by this point and after the sixth operation failed to sort me out I was sick of the situation. The guy I was staying with was a taxi driver and was a mate of Benno, but because I was sleeping on his sofa during the week it was no standard of living. I spent most of my time at his local social club killing time and perhaps the only good thing about the situation was that I was just round the corner from Lords so I got in touch with Mike Roseberry and once managed to blag my way into the Long Room.

Other than that highlight I was sick of my life down there. We'd had the twins but Sonia was having problems with the kids and was struggling too, so I approached Gerry Francis, who had taken over from Roy, and said that I wanted out. He actually tried to change my mind and stop me, but it was madness given the state I was in. I still had time on my contract and he wanted me to give it another go, but I wasn't willing to keep picking up my wage when really I was of no use to them and saw no signs of getting better.

Gerry was brilliant about it and respected my decision. He even offered me a full time coaching job but with the kids back at home it was not going to work out so I went to see one of the directors with my accountant and explained the situation. He was as good as gold with me and very honest, but because the club were not in a position to pay me any compensation for coming out of the contract early I would either have had to take on that coaching job or tear the thing up.

Fortunately I had a personal insurance policy that I'd taken out myself and because

I had that to fall back on I was happy enough to do that, although even that proved to be a bit of a long drawn out process because the company I had gone with had the cheek to suggest I was somehow faking the whole thing, but believe me it was the last thing I wanted to do.

The whole saga went back to when I first left Sunderland; it was the worst decision I could have made, but hindsight is no good to you at the time. You never know what would have happened, but had I suffered a similar problem at Sunderland they would have been in a better position to look after me and I would have still been at home with everybody around me. Even then, when I did call it a day Sacko was the first one on the phone wanting to help me out and whilst it meant the world to me, even that was a sign that I'd been too hasty turning my back on Sunderland.

Sacko wanted to get the club to put me through my coaching badges and all of this so he told me to go and see Ian Branfoot, who was in charge of the academy. Branfoot didn't know me though and the job he offered me was a mickey take, and because I wasn't going to go and brown nose Reidy just to try and get something else that was the end of it.

My time in professional football was up and I packed in aged just 30. It had been 13 years since I had made my debut against Southend United and it was rarely a smooth ride from that point onwards. Most players my age would have still had a good few years left in them, but now I was starting a new chapter in my life.

Durham City provided me a second career in the game

CHAPTER SIXTEEN

New beginnings at New Ferens

It had been in the back on my mind as a player that I would have liked to have gone into coaching, but when nothing came of my conversations with Ian Branfoot I left it at that and decided to look after the children full time while Sonia went to work instead.

I'd been away from my kids so much during my career that this was something I felt was important for me to do, so we leased a hair dressing salon and did it up so Sonia had that to concentrate on whilst I took care of Liam, Charlie and Jess. Liam was only four and the twins were still babies, and having now gone through it first hand I honestly feel bringing up kids is the hardest job anybody can have in the world, never mind a bloke that had just finished football and wasn't used to it on a day to day basis.

I loved the kids more than anything but having year old twins and an older one that wasn't sleeping properly was far from easy. I was doing nappy changes, feeding; the lot, I was hands on and whilst it was hard work I got a routine sorted out. Being a former footballer though I did get the odd funny look from people on the street if I was going somewhere with them all and if I went to a play area or whatever and the place was full of mothers I would feel out of place a lot.

For me, it is true when former footballers say that one of the biggest things you miss when you stop playing is the daily banter you used to have with your team mates. My life was so much different now and it was a culture shock, but I made sure that I still kept in touch with both the mates I had grown up with and some of the lads that were still in the game. About a year after quitting Quinny invited me over to Ireland, and of course Aidy ended up putting a big trip together for all of the boys.

Quinny had bought a bar in Clonmel and wanted us there for the opening so we all flew over to Dublin and when we got there were looking for the bus driver, who was meant to have a sign with 'Big Aidy' on it. We couldn't see him anywhere though and Aidy was getting worked up because I had made on that I had lost the bag with all of our money in. All the lads had paid up front and there was about four or five grand in this holdall so he wasn't best pleased with me messing about, and then when he saw this bloke with a sign with '80' in big digits he knew it was going to be one of those trips.

We checked into our hotel and there were three or four to a room, but they only had two beds each! I was in with the Sunderland physio Gordon Ellis and Bobby Knoxall so we were planning on letting Bobby having a bed to himself, but he wouldn't have it and insisted on sleeping on the floor even at his age, just because he thought my back would go if I didn't have a bed to myself. Come the first night though and I wake up to find him smoking under his bed sheets, he could have had us all alight!

Bobby was winding Aidy up loads because we'd been put on the fourth floor of this hotel, and it took him ages to get up the stairs. He kept telling Aidy "I'm meant to be a star you know" and making a joke of everything, but deep down I think he knew he was in poor health and he stayed away from alcohol throughout the trip and just stuck to tea or coffee. It didn't stop him creasing everybody else up though, nor did anybody else stay off the drink for that matter.

During our first full day there we took part at a charity golf day at Charlesland Golf Club near Bray. Everybody was stotting at the end of the course because we were drinking all the way through so come the dinner afterwards all the other guests were taking it seriously whilst we were messing about. Quinny stood up in this white suit looking like someone out of Daktari and was giving it six nowt about how much had been raised for charity, and then some bloke started speaking Irish so we were all scratching our heads wondering what he was saying. Next to say a few words though was Bobby, and he stole the show.

The place was packed with all of these important Irish personalities such as the President and Vice President, and some of the top clergymen. Then there was a load of celebrities on top of that too, so Quinny had spoken to Bobby before and told him the drill; no swearing, no Irish jokes, that sort of thing. Bobby just kept saying "I'm a pro son, I'm a pro, don't you worry about a thing" and yet the first thing he did when he got up was start hammering them all about the potato famines, and people didn't know whether to shake their heads or burst out laughing.

Then he saw one of the senior priests and had a bit of a craic on with him, but he'd spotted that the ladies captain kept hitting her husband with her handbag because he was laughing so he started on her instead. She wasn't best pleased but he kept coming back at her with all of these quick one liners and in the end everybody in the room was crying with laughter, even Quinny.

We got up the next day and went to the Curragh Racecourse. Quinny had said to us beforehand that he had sorted hospitality tickets for us, but then he saw the state of us in the morning he suddenly decided "right, it's downstairs in the stalls today". Once the racing was over though Pricey came out of nowhere with "ha'way Dickie, I'll give you a race over the final furlong" and even though we were in our suits we hopped over the barrier onto the course and went for it.

The stands were still chocka with punters and once they spotted what we were up to they all started cheering us on. I don't think they had a clue who I was; in their eyes they probably just saw two daft lads running along the Curragh and were getting into the spirit of it. I'd given Pricey a head start but because of my knee I soon realised that I wasn't going to catch him up so I shouted at him to slow down and when I got to the end we held hands and jumped over the finish line together and the crowd just went up, it was hilarious.

After that we got on the bus and went over to Clonmel. Quinny's bar was not opening officially until the next evening but we went in, just to make sure everything was in order of course, and didn't leave until about three o'clock in the morning. We were still up bright and early for another game of golf though and that was another laugh. Quinny's mate Joe Hayes was with us but when him and Pricey came out of the clubhouse there was only one golf buggy left and it was meant to be reserved for the Father from the next village.

Joe was a big name in hurling so when he pointed to Pricey and said "well, I just happen to have the Father with me" they believed him, even though he looked nothing like a man of the cloth! There was a bit of divine intervention in the end though; as because it was that hot Joe decided that they would completely take the mick so him and Pricey came up on the 18th hole wearing only their underpants, but they then realised that Pricey's trousers had fallen off the back of the buggy and when they went back to fetch them they were nowhere to be found.

We were all reasonably sober at this point and one or two of us thought that they had actually gone a bit too far, but then we couldn't help but laugh when Joe started up saying "you shouldn't have taken the Fathers buggy, otherwise the Lord would have left your trousers alone" and Pricey was going "but it was your idea!". He'd had his passport and money in them and we still don't know where those trousers went to this day, not that he seemed that bothered in the end because we were all laughing so much.

The pub was called The Local Bar and it opened that night so we had another good drink before heading off to the hurling the following day. Joe had sorted us all out with tickets and the atmosphere was unbelievable, but of course Quinny became the main attraction as soon as people clocked him; we were stood behind the goal posts and everybody in the stand was chanting his name. We were all pestering him about the rules of the game though, asking him daft questions and in the end he told us all to shut up. We all left it then for a few minutes and then just as he was calming down I pointed to the two Umpire's behind the goal with their white coats on and said "one more question, what are those two butchers doing on the pitch?" and that was it, he didn't speak to us for the rest of the game!

Come the final day we were all wrecked so we just had a few menders in Quinny's pub and left it at that, but it was a great trip. We've been back a few times and always had a real laugh, but I think something about that first trip rubbed off on me because I later took on my own pub for a while; Quinny had made it look easy but I suppose what he did was get the right people in behind the scenes, and by inviting us over he'd made sure they sold enough booze to keep them going for a few months at least!

I think I had about 12 to 14 months totally out of the game, and then when I was having a drink in the Village shortly after getting back from Ireland the gaffer, Big John, jokingly asked me if I would turn out for their Sunday League team. They actually had a good side so I thought 'why not?', but in the end I only got to play once because Gerry Hogan, who is very highly thought of in non league circles, happened to be watching. Hogey got in touch with Brian Honour at Durham City and told him I might be available; my knee was in a mess and my back was dodgy but I'd kept myself quite fit and was in decent enough shape for the Northern League so he thought it might be worth a go.

Brian rang me and asked me to come through for a meeting with him and the chairman, and that was the first time I met Stewy Dawson. They told me that all they could afford was £50 a week and that wasn't a problem at all, I just felt as if I needed to get back into football in some way and the carrot here was that they had just been given permission to build an indoor football centre next door to New Ferens Park and I could have a job working as a director of coaching.

I wasn't particularly looking for a full time job or anything at that point, but I'd still liked the idea of doing something coaching wise even after the position at Sunderland fell through so when this dropped into my lap it appealed to me straight away. It then turned out that Stewy was looking for investors to put money into the business and I eventually got involved with that too, so there is a bit of security for me; not bad for a chance conversation in the Village.

I made my debut for Durham against Dunston and because there was a bit of rivalry a couple of hundred people were in and I thoroughly enjoyed it. The thing that got me straight away was how everybody at the club was part of a little community, people behind the scenes were all pitching in and it was a real team effort. There were some good young lads too, it was a decent side and whilst I didn't really know Brian before hand he came over very well right from the start. His team talks were always excellent and he was very professional in the way he went about things.

I'd only signed for the second half of the season but during the following 2001-02 campaign we got to the semi final of the FA Vase and that whole run was fantastic; being at Durham was a second chance for me and I was enjoying it. We were going to away games on a coach and staying over at places overnight during the run and it was a little reminder of where I had been during my professional career. It was probably one of my best memories from playing football and when we got knocked out by Whitley Bay I was distraught. I'd been made captain and I was doing it for everybody at the club, they really were all lovely people and I was as upset for them as I was myself when we got beat.

The semi final was two legged but we lost the first game at Hillheads Park 2-1 and there was supposedly three thousand spectators back at New Ferens Park for the second leg, but I bet there was something closer the five thousand in truth. The run had brought good exposure for the club but we couldn't get the goal we needed and it ended 0-0, although at least somebody from the region went on to win the trophy because after getting past us the Bay won the final at Villa Park against a side from Essex called Tiptree United.

Five days after that Vase tie though we had another semi final against Whitley Bay, this time in the Northern Football League Cup. Whilst it wasn't quite on the same scale it was important to us that we picked ourselves up and had something to show for the season after doing so well, so knocking them out to reach the final as we did admittedly came as a bit of a relief. The two league games we had with Whitley Bay that season were both drawn and we finished level on points in the table, so it was frustrating that we couldn't quite nudge past them in the Vase, but we did at least end up with some silverware as a consolation by then winning the League Cup in the final game of the season.

The final was by chance due to be held at Durham that season anyway and we beat Shildon 3-2 with a Golden Goal in extra time. Winning that meant that the following season started with a game against the Northern League champions Bedlington Terriers for the JR Cleator Cup, which was a bit like the Northern League's own Community Shield. Despite the game being at Bedlington we won 3-0, and I was finding that the standard of football in the Northern League was always excellent, and even though I had played professionally I still fell exposed in certain situations due to my injuries. I had young, fit players running around me and as I wasn't able to train fully it was a case of patching me up so I could get through the games. The physio at the time was a young lass called Joanne and she was giving me acupuncture therapy twice a week and that seemed to be helping me out with my back, but my knee was likely to go at any time so in one on one situations I had that little bit of doubt in my mind.

There were one or two occasions where I went to turn and I thought I could feel it about to go, but other than that I was always able to read the game very well so could often stop it getting to that point, and without wanting to sound big headed I could dictate games a fair bit, and of course I was enjoying just the fact that I was playing at all; although I do think that my background made me a target in some ways.

There were a few people who saw me and wanted to make some sort of mark for whatever reason and I remember I actually got sent off at Washington after one lad launched himself with two feet at my bad knee. He ended up lying on top of me and I belted him, but I appealed against my suspension and had to go to the FA in Durham. The fella was a bit of a lunatic and meant to do it, he had even told one of his team mates before the game what he was going to do apparently, but to be fair to them their captain came to the hearing to stick up for me and said that it wasn't my fault. He explained the situation and that summed the Northern League up more than the odd bad apple; it is full of good people.

The Durham lads were always good with me as well; there were never any problems towards me because of who I was before joining them and we had great camaraderie within the changing room, which is important at any level. Micky Taylor was an experienced centre forward, he had been round the block and during the Vase run he scored some unbelievable goals, he was a great finisher and because me and him were the older two with a load of younger lads around us we seemed to be the ones starting all the banter and getting the rest involved.

Having a game of football to look forward too each week again was fantastic, but I have no idea whether or not QPR knew I was playing. It wouldn't have mattered though because there was no way I could have gone back to pro level anyway as my body just wasn't up to it, and then one evening in the later stages of the 2002-03 season I was coming down the stairs when my knee finally went again for good; I hadn't even been noticing much pain at all for a while, but I knew straight away that this was the end of it.

Billy Cruddas was the manager having taken over from Brian and I had no choice but to tell him and Stewy that I needed to pack it in again. It was the right decision I know, but it really upset me because I had left QPR at a relatively young age and had loved being involved again. I had already taken up a few coaching duties whilst still playing though, and would now have to make do with being Crud's assistant.

This came during the period after I had just split from Sonia too so the timing was terrible. I have never been somebody to rest on my laurels though; I've tried to get on with things and now I was again unable to play and had separated from my wife I wanted to try my hand at something else in addition to helping Crud run the team. All of the plans for Soccarena had been passed and now the finance was all in place building work was underway, but that wasn't going to be ready until down the line and so because I'd toyed with the idea of running a bar since seeing Quinny in Ireland, Aidy suggested I take on The Royal George in Shotton to see how I got on.

With Aidy being in the pub trade already he was able to help set me up with a six month lease. I took over in the autumn of 2003 but it turned out to be a mad few months, and I soon found out that it wasn't my game at all. I remember for example getting this Hennessy XO cognac in one time, it was this really high quality brand but I had no idea about pricing so was just selling it for a pound a go. We had all these old guys sitting in the corner getting loaded on the stuff and it was only when Aidy came in and told me that I needed to be selling it at something closer to £20 just to maintain my gross profit that I realised I had done anything wrong!

I wasn't the only one in there new to the scene either. I thought we should put a couple of good looking girls behind the bar so we got these two absolute film stars in, but it soon turned out that they'd never pulled a pint before in their lives; Aidy came in one time with Quinny and they ordered their drinks, yet these two girls didn't have a clue what to do next.

We were really busy at first and business was booming, but once the initial rush died off I just seemed to go from one problem to the next. The chef we brought in for example just seemed to do what he wanted but nine times out of ten I was too nice and just let him get away with it, and yet on the one occasion I had to have a word and tell him to buck his ideas up he threatened to hit me so we ended up getting into a fight, and if that wasn't enough to be dealing with it wasn't long afterwards that a couple of lads tried to break in and swipe the takings.

There was a fella called Red Ken though that used to get in and as I was happy to just leave him to finish his drink at the end of the night I would go upstairs without locking the doors. Ken looked liked he was half dead at the best of times and had fallen asleep this one evening, so then when these lads came in and disturbed him he sat bolt upright and started groaning because he didn't know where he was, but these two got the shock of their life and ran out screaming!

Really, the place needed some proper money spending on it to bring it up to scratch and once the novelty wore off and I realised how much of my time it was taking up I lost interest and my Mam and Dad ended up helping me a fair bit until the lease was up. Pratty would pop over a lot to raise my spirits too and we would have a laugh, but I wasn't cut out to run a pub or handle the political side with the brewery and I don't think it's something I'll want to try again unless somewhere special to me like the Village became available. Had it been a success I think I might have kept it on or perhaps taken over somewhere with a bit more potential, but by April 2004 Soccarena was about to open and the time was right to knock it on the head.

Regrettably, with time also finally being called on my relationship with Sonia too, all my attention was now focused on Durham City again and the soon to be open Soccarena.

Still involved; coaching grass roots football is my passion now

CHAPTER SEVENTEEN
Pointless times

When Soccarena opened it was the first indoor six a side arena in the north east and we had made sure the surface was the best in the country by looking at other places all over Europe. One of the other shareholders was Jim Pearson, who played for Newcastle United and had helped open similar centres in other parts of the country for Dave Whelan, but the main man behind it was Stewy Dawson.

Stewy was Chairman next door at Durham City and whilst the two have always been technically separate they go hand in hand in a lot of respects. Stewy used to work for Sunderland at one time when he ran the lottery with Corny O'Donnell and he got involved with Durham when they were at the original Ferens Park. The ground was down at the Claypath area of the city so the land was quite valuable and when developers came in he ended up with the patch of land where the new ground and the football centre is now. Austin Carney is another director at the centre and he now is Chairman of the club, but it was Stewy that gave me the initial opportunity and I'll always be grateful to him for that because I think it has proven to be a bit of a calling.

I feel at home around the place; Soccarena is full of good people and I have made true friends in people like Richie Rodden, Tel Smiles, Paul Taylor, John Anderson and Rhys Jobling; or 'little Dick' as he became known because he was always following me around! These lads are just as close to me as the lads were back in my playing days; Chris Copeland is another one; he used to play for Durham City under me and Crud and has now worked himself up within Soccarena to a position where he and Stewy know what they are doing and can plan for the future. For me though, I stay away from the business side of things and concentrate on the day to day running of the centre and all of the coaching because that is what excites me.

The Soccarena is a busy place and I oversee the Academy sides; there are 20 now in the Russell Foster League going from seven year olds to under 21s and in addition to them I run two sides as part of our contract with Durham Gilesgate College. Seeing all these kids develop is brilliant, it might sound funny to some people but they are like sons to me in many ways; and to see them come on not only as footballers but as people as well is very rewarding.

The college lads are all on a BTEC National Diploma in Sport and looking to work within sport in some way. In many cases they have ended up doing something at Soccarena, but others have gone on to University in America for example or become P.E. teachers and my remit is to look after the football side of things whilst the teachers take care of the academic aspects of the course. We have a couple of training sessions a week and then a game in either the North East Colleges League or the English Colleges Football League and they all love it.

It goes back to that community thing again; it is like a little neighbourhood in itself around Durham City and Soccarena, where everybody looks after each other. For me, doing everything connected with it feels really worthwhile, but of course on a wider scale the college connection pretty much saved the club too when things started to go wrong in 2009.

Going back to Durham City, my involvement was increasing again after leaving the pub and working under Crud was a great introduction to it all. Crud had been in charge when Durham won their first Northern League title in 1994 and he was the best I ever heard in terms of motivation and that includes my time as a professional.

He knew the game too though, so spoke a lot of sense and when he first asked me to help him out and start having a few words with the team before games I was concerned that I wouldn't be able to follow him.

At first I found it hard to even speak out loud, which was strange because they were all just young lads really and I'd had no problems getting involved with the jokes and what have you. As a player I had always been one to speak up in the changing rooms if it were needed too, but because Crud was so thorough it was rare that I would have anything to add; but then he started asking me to step in from the start of team talks and it grew from there up to a point where I was a manager in my own right and I could do it without giving it a second thought - I just planned what I wanted to say tactics wise and the rest came naturally.

Crud was a brilliant mentor for me, but as a partnership we did well too I feel and when we both left the club in February 2005 it is important to point out that we did it for non footballing reasons because we both loved that side of things. Crud was finding it hard to put up with some of the political things going behind the scenes at the club though, whereas I was having a few issues at home since splitting up with Sonia.

We'd first separated in 2003 before I took over the pub but after that we tried a couple of times to patch things up and I lost the plot a little bit I must admit. No longer being in professional football was harder to take than I thought; when I was with the kids and playing the family man I was fine but if they had gone to bed or were with Sonia for the day I felt useless and would just end up drinking to fill the time, and whilst that wasn't the reason we got divorced it certainly didn't help the situation.

When Sonia and I had first got married she helped me settle down a bit and mature but we'd drifted apart later in the relationship and I think now that we were never really that compatible in the first place, as I was more of a laid back character than her and so we'd end up fighting like cat and dog. Sometimes I wonder if I made a mistake by not marrying Nicola but the kids mean everything to me so it was the right decision in that respect and the way Liam, Jessica and Charlie have come through all the changes, the different houses and everything else has been a credit to them.

My childhood had been so good that I always wanted a similar environment for my own kids, but it hasn't happened and that is very regrettable. I wouldn't wish a situation like that on anybody, but the kids have coped with everything and are turning out to be not just lovely children to me but lovely people too. I am now with someone called Susan who is lovely, and we seem more comfortable too, we are both free to do things when we need and it works for us; but at the time I left Durham I felt that I needed to concentrate on family matters.

Although I was no longer officially involved with Durham though, I still knew everything that was going on because the lads would come into Soccarena and keep me up to date. For once the club had quite a large budget but results just wouldn't come and in late October 2006 Stewy asked if I was willing to come back and run the side on a caretaker basis until a new manager was found. There was already a really good squad there and because I knew the problems the players were having I was able to come in and help pick up the results very quickly.

We beat Dunston in my second game and a month later thrashed Ashington. In between that we progressed in the FA Vase and in total won ten our 17 remaining games of the calendar year. We went from a position where some of the lads were coming to me at Soccarena and moaning about the last guy in charge to now, where we had pulled away from the relegation zone of Division One and the mood amongst the squad was great.

In December I agreed to take the job on for the rest of the season, but I felt as if I needed a bit of experience by my side though so I got Lee Collings in from Sunderland Nissan to be my assistant. Lee was from Murton too and although he was in the year above me we played football together at school, and he was someone that knew the non league scene inside out. We continued to do well but by spring time I was having more trouble at home and because the kids wanted me to take them to watch Sunderland on weekends I had to make the decision to pass the reigns to Lee fully.

The more I was doing it, the more management seemed to suit me and had I been in a different situation I doubt I would have left at that point. The family had to come first though, and I felt confident enough that Lee would be able to take the lads on so I spoke to Stewy and told him the situation. The squad I left needed very little in terms of coaching in truth, it was made up of some of the best and most experienced players in the region, and under Lee they won back to back promotion into the Northern Premier League Premier Division after winning the Northern League and then the Northern Premier League Division One North.

That first summer after stepping down I was invited to take part in a charity cricket match at Durham County Cricket Club's Riverside ground and now I had no football in the way I was delighted to be picking a bat up again for the first time in a good 18 years. The match was billed as an 'All Star Twenty20' game between sides representing the Duke of Northumberland and the Earl of Durham and it all came straight back to me; I hit 60 odd and it felt great.

Being able to start playing cricket again regularly would have been fantastic, but I knew that even that could have been too much for my body so the game had to be a one off and a nice way to remember an enjoyable part of my childhood. Instead I concentrated on the Soccarena and with Durham City now playing at level seven of the football league pyramid I would still go to watch games at New Ferens if I was not at Sunderland with the bairns. The club were looking to progress even further up the system and were budgeting accordingly having sold their plan to different sponsors and backers, but come the 2009-10 season everything went down the swanny and that was when the college lads came along to save the day.

The club had installed an artificial pitch in conjunction with Soccarena and the income it brought into the football club was very important. Bookings could be taken from all sorts of groups and other clubs all day every day without their being any damage done to the pitch, and the fact that games were not getting called off over the winter meant Durham didn't have fixture pile ups to worry about at the end of the season, so in those respects the pitch was a great idea.

Some FA competitions did not allow the use of the surface though and even during my time as manager if we were drawn at home in the something like the Vase the tie would have to be switched to a neutral venue. The club had been led to believe however that it would not prevent them from trying to move up the levels, until the start of the season that is when the Football Conference announced that it was not the case, affectively putting a ceiling on how high the club could go.

Within a very short space of time the club's main sponsor had pulled out, and with the players no longer getting paid they were soon cherry picked by other teams in the area. It meant the club had to put together a side from scratch just days before the season was due to start and were forced to call upon the college side. Lee asked me to come back too and we worked for nothing alongside these kids just so the club could fulfil their fixtures.

Although the boys were all talented players they were raw too and went from playing against similar aged teams to being thrown in at the deep end against serious men, many of whom were semi professional. We knew we couldn't compete, but the club barely had a pulse and all we were doing was trying to keep it going on a week by week basis.

We were crawling along, taking hit after hit, but not once did the lads let themselves down and their attitude was amazing. They had found themselves in this situation where they had gone from enjoying a bit of football alongside their studies to being labelled 'the worst team in England' and all of that rubbish in the media. It was so unfair because the real story never got out properly, and none of the lads were bad players - it's just that as a team the odds were stacked against them.

A real low point came against Kings Lynn in the November. We lost 11-0 and it could have been more in truth, but the impact it would have on the season was far more wide reaching in the end. Against Bradford Park Avenue and then Kings Lynn we chose to field Joshua Home Jackson under a false name even though he was suspended, purely because we had nobody else. Josh was a former Sunderland Academy and reserve team player and was one of the few lads we had with any experience to speak of, but we were not trying to gain an advantage or anything, we lost the games 7-1 and 11-0 after all, our only intention was to complete the games both for ourselves and our opponents.

It was wrong and we held our hands up. We made the FA aware and were open about everything when they investigated, and as a result we were docked six points and given a fine. Had it been left at that we would have understood, but the club also banned Lee from having any involvement with the club for the rest of season and handed Josh another suspension. Josh had only been doing as he was asked and simply wanted to help out as best he could, so I felt horrible for him to have his name dragged through the mud.

Lee though, he chose to step forward ahead of me and take the rap. We expected him to get a short touch line ban or something similar and he perhaps felt it would be better if I was available because the lads were all my college kids, but for him to then not be allowed anywhere near games at all when the club was already in dire straights felt well over the top. We decided as a group to just take it on the chin though and battle on as hard as ever, although now everything was solely down to me.

We lost our first 28 games that season and our first victory of the campaign in March 2010 was one of the best moments of my career as a manager. Any win would have been brilliant, but we managed it against FC United of Manchester at Gigg Lane and that made it even better because they were such a good team. Our kids were not used to playing in front of much more than 100 people and yet they went to a Football League ground and won in front of a couple of thousand, and just as importantly it was fully merited.

Andrew Stevenson scored our winner with a brilliant lob from close to the half way line, and our keeper Rhys 'Little Dick' Jobling saved a last minute penalty just to make it all the more sweeter. For him that was fantastic because before that we had already conceded over 100 goals in the season and for a goalkeeper to see so many goals fly past him each week must have been soul destroying. I let the players have their moment on the pitch and sloped off to the dressing rooms but I was so emotional I ended up having a big bubble to myself; not the first time a game at Gigg Lane had caused me to cry!

As often happens in football, after waiting for so long to get our first win, the second one came straight after when we beat Whitby Town at home a couple of days later. Due to the points deduction though all those wins did was get us back to zero, and as we ended up losing our remaining games we ended the season pointless. At least though we had got to grips with things a bit more and in our last few games sides had to work really hard just to beat us by one or two.

Daft as it sounds though, even after all of that it wasn't until well into the summer that our relegation back into the Northern Premier League First Division North was confirmed as a lot of other clubs had landed in financial bother too. A number of other clubs in the non league scene went to the wall during this period so the simple fact we were still in existence was a plus point, and it was all thanks to those lads who kept getting up off the floor again and again to allow the board time to pull the finances round.

Austin was now chairman and with the hard work of him and the rest of the club we were able to get a bit of a budget together for the 2010-11 season to make sure we were able to compete, although we were still going to have to rely heavily on the college lads. Some of the group had left their studies but wanted to stay on at Durham and with me and Lee now working together as joint managers we ended the season in a credible 17th position. Still though, without any major income things were always tight and our job was to just try and rush the kids through whilst the board tried to keep us afloat.

The 2011-12 season saw Lee leave his post and I was back in charge by myself. Lee and I had started to disagree about how we should move forward, as he wanted to try and use the little money we did have to bring in a couple more experienced players, but I didn't feel comfortable ditching the boys that had stuck by us just to finish a couple of places higher in the table. Besides, you could see the players getting better all the time and I would always try to drum into them that making mistakes was okay as long as they learned from them.

The decision to let Lee go was right I feel, but the way I went about it was wrong and I still regret it now. I tried to tell him to his face a couple of times and I nearly ended up in tears so in the end I texted him and asked him to come and see me, but he knew what was going to happen so didn't bother and I haven't seen him since to clear the air. I feel that it was the best for all concerned that he went, but I wish I had done it differently. His ideas were different to mine and I knew it would end in tears so I wanted to try and avoid that, but in the end it didn't work out like that. No doubt I will bump into him and we can sort it but I do feel bad about it even now.

After such a bleak couple of years however we ended up having a solid season. The club had started to get some new members involved with the committee and had attracted a couple more sponsors, and with everybody pulling in the right direction we spent a lot of the time near the play off zone, and I even managed to pick up the Manager of the Month award for October. Sadly though, instead of being handed a bottle of something by way of a prize I was given a rain jacket and a polo shirt from the league sponsor and whenever I wore them the lads just took the mick!

We ended up in 9th place with a pretty even record of 20 wins, 20 defeats and 2 draws, with 81 scored and 80 conceded and I think we could have improved further over time, but with so many of our opponents based in the North West the travelling was always an issue so myself and several other people within the club had been pushing the idea of us dropping down in the Northern League again.

In football you want to be at the highest level possible, but not if it is going to cost the club in the long run and not if it takes some of the fun away. We seemed to be up and down the M62 every other week because the sides all seemed to be from the Manchester and Liverpool areas and it took a lot out of the players and the club's finances, so I'd felt for a long time we'd be more competitive were we in a local league and using our resources differently. We agreed then to go back to the

Northern League for the 2012-13 season, but rather than see this as a backwards step it should make the club stronger and the football more enjoyable; and having now got to that point with Durham still in one piece I have decided to step aside as manager.

Over the years I have had to come and go a few times, but I have loved it and whilst Durham City will always be my club I have reached a point where all the hard work and tears were taking their toll and I need to ease off. The link with Soccarena is as strong as ever and hopefully there will be an opportunity for the college kids to still be brought through to the club, but a new man might liven things up and because games are all on the doors the atmosphere should be a lot better for a start. Durham might see a few more away fans turning up and as games will now have a bit of local interest there should be a bit of spice to them, so whilst deciding to go was not an easy option I truly hope that things will continue to improve for the club.

When I first joined people used to see us as a big club and a team to beat. Tommy Porter, the old Sunderland groundsman, used to look after our pitch so we had the best surface around, but because of that teams would assume that we had money and were the big boys so wanted to put one over us. People will be looking to do the same now because Durham City have been playing higher up the system, but one or two of the more senior players have left and the club needs to start from scratch again, and that is something I feel needs to be done by somebody who is able to see it through.

Teams like Spennymoor and Whitley Bay are from big towns and they get big crowds, and Darlington are in there too, headed up by my old Sunderland pals Martin Gray, Tony Norman and Brian Atkinson. Not many England Under 21s will have found their way down to management in level nine of the football pyramid I would have thought but it is an indication of the standard of the Northern League now. Things might not be easy, but this is a new era now for Durham.

Surveying the scene...

CHAPTER EIGHTEEN

The good Ord days

At Durham we would usually train two nights a week and then have a Saturday or midweek game. We didn't have a reserve team and I didn't have to go scouting players all that often because they usually come through the college or had made us aware that they are available, so I would spend a lot of time thinking about the games themselves instead or on the phone organising and taking care of the administration side.

The worst aspect of the job was if I had to drop somebody; I stressed a lot about it before hand, but would always make a point of telling them to their face because having them find out via a team sheet on the wall does them no good, as I know myself. I would pull them to one side and tell them personally, and that was very hard because of the connection I have with most of them, but by doing it that way and explaining the reasons they could at least work on the issues.

I tried not to be the type of manager that is forever screaming and shouting at players either; during games I was busy taking it all in so only ever turned up the volume as a shock option, otherwise it loses any impact. For me, management is mainly about encouragement and organising the team though, or certainly that is how I tried to be and how I think it should be, what ever the level.

Having been involved in football all this time didn't do anything to help me with my nerves though and if anything I was getting worse before games than I ever did as a player. Managers would always say to me that when you are responsible for a side and taking all the flak it is harder to be watching on and only being able to have a limited impact than it is actually being out there, and of course it is only now that I understand how true this is.

I truly mean it when I say the squad and the club felt like family to me, so I got chewed up before games just as much as I would do in my playing career. Even when I was doing well I would get short tempered and grumpy before games; I wanted to do well for everybody else as much as for myself and I felt the same way with Durham. Every player or manager will tell you though that once the whistle blows and you realise you are in familiar surroundings you are suddenly at your most comfortable, whether it is at school boy level or in front of thousands of people, and the pay off comes when you win; because that feels like nothing else.

The non league scene is unbelievable at the moment; the passion from those running the clubs is immense and the different characters you meet are fantastic. Non league today is more like the game that I fell in love with, people are passionate and wanted to win, but they can have fun too. There is still a bit of a drinking culture, or at least at Durham there was anyway, and the social side was what made it for me; we would always have a drink after training or on the bus back from an away match and the lads were always going out on the town together as a group, although believe it or not I had to admit that I am getting a bit old for that now and couldn't hack it anymore!

It is important to these lads that they win though and the lower levels have got more professional as time has gone on. Sports science has progressed a lot for example, and the knowledge Durham's physio Gary Miller has is unbelievable; in fact had the human body been understood as much in my time it could have helped my own career a whole load. Steve Smelt, my physio at Sunderland, knew his stuff, but things move on and now we are at a point where even the non professional game is more advanced than when I was at the top.

I do get asked if I would like to get back into the professional game and if Owersy got an offer somewhere I might consider working as a coach under him, but I have to be honest and say that I don't particularly like it the way it is as the moment. Take my own coaching with the younger age groups, we try to make it fun but I think the academies are signing some kids on when they are far too young and instead of allowing them to enjoy their football and their childhood and learn naturally, they are put under pressure to produce straight away.

The plan now is to keep learning and see what it brings - I wouldn't even rule out a return to Durham City at some point given our history! It took me ten years to get my UEFA B Coaching Badge and when I passed in early 2012 the first thing I did was ring Owersy and tell him that I wanted to do the A Badge. My assessor encouraged me to do it too and as Gary said to me, I now 'have the bug'. The ten years bit is a bit of a joke really though; Sacko put me on the course when it looked like I was going to get a coaching job at Sunderland but when that fell through I didn't follow it up until I was at Durham.

I'm not intending taking so long with this one; although it does need dedication. The badges require you to attend residential courses and complete work books, but you have to put the hours in on the training pitches too and that means the different college and kids' sides will benefit from this as well. I don't just think I know it all because I have played the game; although naturally I do bring some elements across and it is ironic that it was Sacko that first put me onto this path because he is the one person I try and follow the most.

Sacko is a legend in my eyes, and as a bloke you couldn't beat him. The team spirit we had when he and Reidy were together was amazing, but I don't think you have that so much within the game now and that is a real shame. Even when things were not always going well before Reidy arrived there were daft things that would keep you going; The Charlie Hurley Centre at Whitburn seemed like the coldest place on earth when you were training sometimes but we would just end up taking the mick out of Benno because the colour of his knees would change in bad weather. In was always just daft fun though, and I don't know if current players have that camaraderie anymore.

I'm not bitter and I don't begrudge anybody that makes a good living from the game if they have put the work in though, but speaking as a fan first and foremost some of the changes I have seen take place sadden me. Players are put on a pedestal; you have to go through three or four people just to get to talk to them and I think it is wrong because some of them lose touch with reality and think they are something different, they forget who helped get them there.

One of the other big things is that sides used to have several local lads in them and at Sunderland players like Bally, Benno and Quinny ended up as adopted Mackems if you will. I don't see that as much now and whilst expansion is good in some ways, if fans cannot relate to players the connection will die. People will switch off, not so much those that go now because it is habit, but will they be as keen to take their kids however?

Parents may think twice about getting their kids into something that seems out of control or too distant and one of the things I hope comes across in this book is that I was playing at a time football was improving but had not gone too far the other way. I was privileged to play football but I didn't expect to be treated like royalty. Some players at the top level no longer mix in the same circles as the fans though and if the bubble bursts I don't know how the game will go.

It is easy to see what has caused it all though; money. Football is an entertainment so players deserve a good wage I feel, but the levels we have now prevent them having any bond with the clubs and attracts too many dodgy characters into the running of the game.

The game has changed for supporters too, obviously tickets cost a lot more and the fact that top flight grounds are all seater mean you don't have that same sort of intense atmosphere that would get people hooked; even now I can still remember seeing us get promoted against West Ham in 1980 - because we couldn't get into our usual spot Dad had to squeeze us into the Clock Stand, but the mood was still unbelievable for a kid like me.

I hear people say that there aren't the characters in the game either, that played to win but had something about them. John Kay is the best example, my Mam was always particularly fond of him and the stories I could tell about him would fill a book by themselves but he was one of a dying breed, a lot of players now have to be clean cut because they have signed away image rights or whatever, and it is another sad reflection on the way things are.

I do admit that older players and fans will always look back and think things were better in their day, but I honestly feel that I wouldn't enjoy playing in this era as much. I probably had the best of both worlds because players were fairly well paid but the game was still true to its roots. I experienced the social side too and played when the game was fun, so I see no reason to be jealous the way some ex pros are. I can understand how somebody that used to be at the top can see relatively average players making millions these days and feel short changed, but in my eyes that's life; you go with the times and whilst I had my fair share of ups and downs the memories will always mean something to me.

I got my break fairly young and soon learned how odd football can be. Things that appear bizarre to a fan looking on in from the outside soon seem normal to you and you have to learn how to handle change; you might be a team mate of somebody for years and then one day they leave and you never see them again, and at a place like Sunderland where I was under so many different managers you were never settled for long. Some of these chapters must read like a potted history of the club as much as they do my own story, but I was there during a turbulent period and they were all major parts of my life.

It seems obvious to say, but the club really did change almost beyond recognition. For long periods though I felt we just drifted along, but that was not for the players to query; things at board room level were kept away from you and as players you just had to get on with your job and keep yourself to yourself. We were in a position where as long as a new contract was going to be put on the table you didn't go asking too many questions, but things are totally different now; the change of stadium has made everything else you see now at Sunderland possible. The club has established itself in the top flight and is known across the world, watched by millions of people on TV and playing pre season games in far flung places like South Korea.

The furthest I ever went with the first team was Norway in 1994 and we were that bored we all grew beards. We were in caravans and there was nothing to do, nowhere to go, and the closest we ever got to a wider audience was when we were live on Tyne Tees over a Sunday lunch time. Live football was still fairly new at that level and a lot was made of how we struggled in front of the cameras, but I think it was more just the fact we were in poor form anyway as opposed to it being on telly that was the issue. It certainly wasn't something I was ever conscious of, I could focus on the match itself and if I did something wrong like the time I got sent off against Middlesbrough it was only afterwards that it registered.

The only time I ever did anything on purpose was also against Boro actually, I knew Gary was going to be watching with all of his new Bristol City mates so I told him

I would give him a sign and when we were lining up in the tunnel I slapped the back of my head for a laugh. On the pitch though I wanted to play the games like any other and it was only when we got to the Premiership that being on TV became more of a regular occurrence and we ended up at a point where match going fans were being inconvenienced too much. It is another issue the game has because whilst it brings in the money, having football on every day of the week comes at a cost to the traditional fan base.

Newspapers too started covering football much more during my playing days, and that lead to me getting my own column in the Sunderland Echo when we where in the Premiership. It wasn't something I had thought about wanting to do, but Graeme Anderson rang me and asked if I fancied it and I thought it was a good chance to try and connect more with the fans. I was able to go into a bit more depth than I could in a normal interview and I suppose it showed that I'd become one of the more senior players.

It was interesting doing something different like the column, but that wasn't my only claim to fame that season because I had a single released about me too! The 'Who needs Cantona' chant was released by Simply Red and White, who were the same people behind 'Cheer Up Peter Reid' the year before and had performed at my Testimonial Dinner at Rainton Meadows. You can still download it from iTunes or listen to it on YouTube if you want, and I have to admit that whilst it was only a bit of fun having a song is a nice thing to be able say about yourself.

In fact, the original chant got dragged out again in January 2012 when Sunderland were playing away at Peterborough United in the FA Cup. The fans were airing all the old songs and because the game was live on ITV I was sitting at home watching when all of sudden they were singing about me. I have to say that it was good to be remembered like that, and fans are always good with me now; public speaking is not something that comes easily to me but if people approach me in a bar or at the Soccarena in small groups I love talking to them or giving them an autograph and hopefully it means they appreciated how much I wanted to win for them.

If I am ever asked to describe myself as a player I joke on and say slow, but deep down I would like to be thought of as somebody that always gave 100% effort. I must have had a little bit of skill I guess, but I was determined more than anything else and I wanted to win for Sunderland at all costs. The only aspect of playing the game that I didn't enjoy was having to be wary of somebody racing through, because whilst I joke about being slow in truth it was an issue. It was always in the back of my mind that I wasn't the quickest and I didn't want to get caught out in a one on one situation so it was always the case that I would make sure I read things as best I could.

Perhaps a bigger problem for me though was not a physical issue, but between my ears, because I honestly feel that my lack of confidence had a major impact on me for a number of years. I had a great introduction into the game but after falling out of Denis' plans I never really got back to an acceptable level mentally until Reidy came and put an arm round me. Things were improving to an extent under Butch and Mick, but I was always being shifted about by them and Crossa, and nobody spoke to me or talked me through my problems.

From a wider point of view, if you think that three of four managers could come along after Smith and still not fix the problems with me, it is easy to see why the club did not go forward in the way it wanted; I wouldn't have been the only player not being utilised properly and if three or four players in a side are suffering with confidence issues and not feeling comfortable it will show in the overall performance even if the players themselves don't even recognise what they are feeling. It's a point I keep making, but that is how Reidy turned things around with a squad of mainly the same players; man management.

We always had a good social life during my days at Sunderland and it was done at the right time, but looking back I know some might feel it possibly was too much. Attitudes are different now, footballers can be pretty much tee total during the season, but when I joined I went from being a timid kid uninterested in drinking to being an 18 year old with my first house, partying every weekend. There was even a time when I was approached by an old lady in the street asking me to sign a petition to 'get Richard Ord off our estate!'

As it happens I just returned to the top end of Murton near the end of 2011, so I'm back to my roots. Since splitting up with Sonia I have been all over and spent the year before living with Susan and her son in Hetton Downs, but now I have my own place again my kids are free to come and go as they please. The house itself is oldish, but it has nothing to do to it so that is it for me, no more moves I hope.

When I was still at Sunderland I moved to a converted farm house in Hetton le Hill and I turned the garage into a snooker room with all of my memorabilia up on the wall, it was a proper boys room and we would have parties in there all of the time too, but things change and you have to settle down; so hopefully I wont be seeing any more petitions in my new place!

I now just want to have a few holidays on the beach and be able to see the kids as much as possible. Pratty and I still like to get away with the boys and Susan and I go away together as well; I love getting a bit of sun and I see the bairn's loads. Charlie is in one of our Academy teams and plays cricket now for Eppleton, and is already showing a bit of promise. Jess is into her horse riding, which is quite sporty too. She has a horse up at Haswell Farm and has won a range of rosettes from different gymkhanas.

Liam meanwhile has drifted away from cricket of late but is at college and funnily enough has signed up for Durham City, so at least there will still be one Ord involved with the club now that I've left. I always had to be careful with him because I didn't want to show him any favouritism but to be fair to him when I did have to say anything he just got on with it.

They all have their interests and I do what I can to support them, because it always meant to world to me if Mam or Dad were on the sidelines supporting me and even up until I left if she wasn't able to be there in person Mam would ring me after a Durham City game to see how we got on.

My back can still have a tendency to give up; and now and again I end up spending a week or so in bed when the pain gets too much. I can't play anywhere near as much golf as I would like either, and football is a no goer; not even five a side. I see people getting stuck in when we have leagues on at Soccarena and wish I could run on and play, but I know the pain would be too much now and even if I go for a run my knee and back are stiff afterwards. If a see a ball laying around the place my instinct still is to kick it though or play a bit of keepy uppy, and whilst I couldn't get involved with the training any longer all the Durham lads still knew I was the best two touch player going, even if they did always claim I was cheating!

I don't get to many Sunderland games these days. I will always be a fan no matter what, but Roker Park was ingrained in me and watching at the stadium doesn't feel quite right. Maybe if I had not actually played at Roker Park so much and had so many strong memories that might not have been the case, because the majority of other fans have embraced the move and if anything it has attracted more supporters to the club.

The other factor keeping me away though is how I left the club; I wish things had worked out differently and going back too often just drags it all up again. I see the injuries and leaving the club as two separate things though, because the knee problems could have happened anywhere at anytime, but certainly I regret leaving when I did because that was where I was meant to be; it was always going to be Sunderland.

I'm not a speaker and I don't always feel comfortable in front of people, but putting this book together has been different and I have enjoyed it. One of the reasons behind doing it was so the bairns and my family would have something to look back on, but is has helped bring a lot of memories back too and so I realise that whilst it wasn't always fun, and there have been lots of ifs and buts in my life, I wouldn't have changed the opportunities I have had for anything.

DEBUT

3 NOVEMBER 1987 · DIVISION THREE · ROKER PARK

Sunderland 7 · 0 Southend United

Scorers: Gates (4), Atkinson (2), Gabbiadini   Attendance: 15,754

LAST GAME

10 MAY 1998 · DIVISION ONE PLAY OFF SEMI FINAL (1ST LEG) · BRAMALL LANE

Sheffield United 2 · 1 Sunderland

Scorer: Ball   Attendance: 23,808

TOTAL APPEARANCES

Sunderland: 256 (plus 28 as a substitute)
York City: 3 (on loan)
England Under 21s: 3

GOALS SCORED

31 DECEMBER 1988 · DIVISION TWO · ROKER PARK

Sunderland 4 · 0 Portsmouth

Scorers: Gates, Ord, Armstrong, Pascoe   Attendance: 21,566

7 JANUARY 1989 · FA CUP 3RD ROUND · ROKER PARK

Sunderland 1 · 1 Oxford United

Scorer: Ord   Attendance: 17,074

18 NOVEMBER 1989 · DIVISION TWO · ROKER PARK

Sunderland 3 · 1 Plymouth Argyle

Scorers: Gabbiadini, Owers, Ord   Attendance: 15,033

28 SEPTEMBER 1993 · DIVISION ONE · ROKER PARK

Sunderland 2 · 2 Grimsby Town

Scorers: Goodman, Ord   Attendance: 15,488

23 OCTOBER 1993 · DIVISION ONE · ROKER PARK

Sunderland 1 · 0 West Bromwich Albion

Scorer: Ord   Attendance: 19,505

24 JANUARY 1996 · DIVISION ONE · ROKER PARK

Sunderland 1 · 0 Grimsby Town

Scorer: Ord   Attendance: 14,656

21 AUGUST 1996 · PREMIERSHIP · CITY GROUND

Nottingham Forest 1 · 4 Sunderland

Scorers: Gray, Quinn (2), Ord   Attendance: 22,874

26 DECEMBER 1996 · PREMIERSHIP · ROKER PARK

Sunderland 2 · 0 Derby County

Scorers: Ord, Russell   Attendance: 22,512

HONOURS

Division Three Champions: 1987·1988

Promotion to Division One: 1989·1990

Division One Champions: 1995·1996

Young Player of the Year: 1988·1989

Player of the Year: 1995·1996

Ending at the start; back to where it began in Woods Terrace